# The TRAINING Remedy

## Making the Most of Teacher Training

**Judy Wortley**

**David C. Cook Publishing Co.**
**Elgin, Illinois—Weston, Ontario**

This manual is dedicated
with thankfulness
to the team that made teacher training happen:
Carol Dias, Janelle Gibbs, Sue Muzny, and Donna Waddell

The Training Remedy

By Judy Wortley

©1991 David C. Cook Publishing Co.

Published by DAVID C. COOK PUBLISHING CO.
850 N. Grove Ave., Elgin, IL 60120
Cable address: DCCOOK
Edited by Gary Wilde
Designed by Russell S. Barr
Cover design by Russell S. Barr
Cartoons by Rob Portlock
Illustrations by Marilee Harrald-Pilz
Art on pages 83-85 courtesy of Dynamic Graphics, Inc., Peoria, Illinois
Printed in the United States of America
ISBN: 1-55513-581-1

# CONTENTS

"I just can't figure out why my volunteers keep quitting on me."

# INTRODUCTION

"Working with kids isn't as much fun as I thought it would be. In fact, some Sundays it's a real pain."

"I think, basically, I'm afraid of those little ones. I become so stressed out when they get out of control. I feel like they are controlling me!"

"Kids today have no respect. I just don't want to be bothered putting up with the hassle."

"I feel like I don't know what I'm doing. I don't know anything about children, so count me out."

"Working with kids wasn't exactly a positive experience. I don't ever want to do that again!"

Excuses, excuses, and more excuses. We hear them all the time. But wait—what's behind those excuses? Do we sense a clear need motivating each excuse we hear? If not, perhaps we should listen a little closer.

Behind the discouragement, fear, anxiety, and inadequacy there is a common theme—lack of proper training. Almost every excuse we hear from those not wanting to become involved, or those quitting after only a short time of teaching or working with children, can be traced back to a volunteer's lack of confidence in his or her ability to carry out the teaching task.

Remember learning to ride your first bicycle? Nervous, sweaty hands? Weaving all over the sidewalks? Scraped knees and elbows? It didn't take very many falls for me to say, "This is it for me. I don't like to have scraped knees. This is too hard."

Trying to learn to ski at the age of forty-five was no picnic, either. I remember vividly that winter morning when my husband said, "I'm going to put you in a course with a great ski instructor and then you will gain confidence quickly." After about three hours on the bunny hill my "great ski instructor," frustrated beyond hope, said, "You are afraid. Just don't be afraid anymore. Let yourself go." Well now, how do I do

This book deals primarily with children's ministry, but the concepts can easily be adapted to training programs that encompass teachers of youth and adult classes.

that? I don't know what I'm doing! Fear, anxiety, discouragement, and feelings of inadequacy quickly set in. I fell down so many times, and ate so much snow, that by the end of the day, I sighed with exasperation, "This is fun? I paid for this fun? I'm never going to do this again!"

But, ask me to teach a Sunday school class and I'll say yes every time! That's because I know what I'm doing and how to do it. Sometimes it's hard for me to imagine that anyone could say, "Teaching is too hard," or, "I just don't know how to work with children." But then I remember my experience on the ski slopes and realize how natural it is for someone who isn't adequately trained to feel that way.

"People tune out if they feel they are failing, because 'the system' is to blame. They tune in when the system leads them to believe they are successful. They learn that they can get things done because of skill, and most important, they are likely to try again. The old adage is 'nothing succeeds like success.' It turns out to have a sound scientific basis. Researchers studying motivation find that the prime factor is simply the self-perception among motivated subjects that they are in fact doing well." (*In Search of Excellence*, Peters and Waterman, Warner Publishers.)

Today, more than ever before, we need to uplift and strengthen our volunteers with the most excellent training we can offer them. People are being stretched beyond their limits. The increasing number of working mothers has definitely taken a toll on the availability of volunteers. Many men are assuming greater responsibilities with the children and home and have less time to volunteer. Entire families are under incredible stress. Thus, it is so necessary for us to realize that when people do consider the sacrifice of doing volunteer work, they need *and want* to be equipped to do the job with the least amount of stress possible. We may be tempted to think that volunteers won't have time for training, but they will find the time if it helps them be successful. In the long run, effective training will save them time and lessen their stress. Training is of utmost importance!

A volunteer secured with solid training is a volunteer that will stand the test of time. To the well-trained volunteer, teaching becomes a life-style. The volunteer who has received good training is not encumbered with the "how to's" of teaching, but has been freed up to love and value the students. He or she has been given the freedom to concentrate on imparting spiritual and moral values, not just facts. The primary goal of our volunteers is to personify Jesus' love to children, youth, and adults. Proper training will free them up to do and be just that.

"Instruct a wise man and he will be wiser still; teach a righteous man and he will add to his learning" (Proverbs 9:9).

# DECIDE

## why you need teacher training

*"Do I need a bigger funnel . . . or a smaller Bible?"*

### When you have taken this step, you will be able to:

- Communicate your philosophy of children's ministry.
- List the benefits of teacher training to yourself and your volunteers.
- Respond to objections workers may have to teacher training.

# Supporting the Case for Teacher Training

Talking with Sunday school superintendents, children's pastors, and children's ministry directors, I often hear the statement, "I find it so unnecessary to have regular teacher meetings. They just aren't that important." Or many say, "My people just won't come to another meeting." They give all kinds of reasons for not holding regular teacher training. From Sunday school teachers I hear, "Why do we need another meeting? I've taught Sunday school for years; I don't need the training." The toughest one is: "I'm a public school teacher, so I know how to teach."

I realize it's very tempting to give up or give in, or even never begin, and just scrap the whole idea of a training program for your volunteers. It seems sort of ridiculous to hold teacher training just to say, "I held teacher training," or "I guess we're supposed to do this." You need to believe in what you are doing so much that nothing can dissuade you from planning and preparing such exciting meetings that workers will look forward to attending.

I want to begin by sharing with you some of the main reasons I found during my ten years as a children's director for having regular teacher training. I want you to capture the vision of what effective training can do for your volunteers.

Teacher training became so necessary to the "success" of my recruiting efforts and keeping my volunteers in place, it took precedence over many other activities. One of my top priorities was regular teacher training. Discouragement sets in quickly when people are untrained in whatever they are doing, whether they are volunteering or being paid. You will be paving the way to longevity in commitment from your volunteers as well as equipping them to do the task at hand with excellence. Let's explore together the reasons we need to have solid training for our precious volunteers.

## Imparting Vision

Every children's pastor, children's director, or Sunday school superintendent needs to be able to impart his or her vision for children's ministry. Volunteers who come into the Sunday school, after-school club, children's church, or any other program should know what the goals for the ministry are and what the ministry stands for. People who understand the primary goal of the ministry will function at a much higher level than those who are just filling space because there was a need.

You must establish a philosophy of children's ministry in your own mind and heart! If you don't know clearly in your mind where you are going and

Every person, no matter how small
the task, needs to feel he or she is
a part of something very special
and significant.

what you want to accomplish, you will find it very difficult to ask someone else to join forces with you in ministering to children. If no one leads, no one will follow.

This philosophy must be the hallmark of your ministry. Every volunteer who works with you must be aware of that philosophy. You need to constantly put this philosophy before the congregation and the staff with which you work—in newsletters, memos, in your conversations with people, and at every training event. Your philosophy statement should be easily stated in one sentence, so that those who work with you, as well as the parents in your congregation, may be able to share that philosophy with others they may bring to church.

It may take several months for you to firmly establish the philosophy and goals of the ministry with your volunteers. A clear and concise philosophy statement will make sharing your desired goals much simpler. In time, every volunteer should be able to answer these questions:

- What is the philosophy of children's ministry in this church?
- Exactly what are we trying to achieve?

Being able to answer those kinds of questions will give volunteers confi-

dence in their ministry as well as help them see a real purpose in working with children. Training events are the ideal forum for communicating your philosophy of children's ministry to your team.

## Building Team Spirit

Every person, no matter how small the task, needs to feel he or she is a part of something very special and significant. "No man is an island" could never be a truer statement than in children's ministry. In children's ministry, being part of a team will make all the difference in your volunteers' ability to avoid burnout. The amount of affirmation flowing from the church body to those working with children is often low. Therefore, being on a team with peers in the teaching task will be a primary source of staying power.

Volunteers left on their own will become very discouraged. For example, people are able to "see" their fellow choir members all in one place at a time. But in children's ministry people usually serve in separate places. So to avoid isolation and the resulting discouragement, it really helps to have a "gathering in" of all those involved. Knowing they are part of an important team, and that adults and children are depending on them, adds a whole new dimension to working with children. As volunteers

> The volunteer who makes this sacrifice should be given other opportunities for fellowship with other believers.

begin to realize they are involved in so much more than just "child care," the excitement of being called to a team of children's ministers will add to their willingness to attend teacher training.

When volunteers function as a team, they become aware of what is happening in their department, and in the ministry as a whole. But they will never see the bigger picture aside from a regular meeting of all those involved in children's ministry. In churches without regular training meetings, most volunteers are not aware of who is working in the next department, or in the Wednesday night group, or in some other program. It is helpful for them to realize how many others are involved in work they are vitally interested in.

Being on a team is much different than playing the game alone. Today we value the idea of a "support group." Why not view teacher training as an opportunity to give your volunteers a support group of their own!

## Offering Encouragement

Working in children's ministry can become a very discouraging task! Often it does not seem as "glamorous" as some of the other ministries people are involved in. The fruit of children's workers' labors are often not evident for many years. The bulk of the congregation may not even realize what teaching goes on in the classroom.

Volunteers often hear unintentionally hurtful comments like: "Oh I had no idea you were teaching; I thought you were just baby-sitting." "I'm certainly glad you take the time to be with the children; somebody's got to do it, I suppose." "Better you than me!" "We sure miss you in the adult study." Yet I've had many volunteers say something like this following a training meeting: "I was so tired tonight after work that I almost stayed home. But I'm so glad I came. I'm all ready for another month. I couldn't do without these meetings. They are so encouraging to me."

Scripture is very explicit about our responsibility to encourage people with good words. "Therefore encourage one another and build each other up, just as in fact you are doing" (I Thess. 5:11).

In ministering to young people there is a unique dynamic that is not prevalent in working with adults. Children's workers do not usually see the fruit of their labors as quickly as those who work with adults, who can respond at the very moment of ministry. With children, it can be months or even years before results are seen. The teacher comes to class prepared to give insight to the Bible truth for the week, and just as he reaches the heart of the issue, a four

*Your workers need confidence . . . ,
and they will only feel that way if
you are also confident that God will
equip you to do your job.*

year old raises her hand and says, "Do you like my new shoes?" Or a fourth grader flies his paper airplane across the room during the application time, just when a teacher is challenging her class to live more like Jesus. Teachers can study all week and see little or no results when the lesson is over. Knowing that others experience these same frustrations can give a real boost to someone who is feeling discouraged.

But there are those moments in teaching when something really neat happens—a child freely offers a hug, someone comes to know the Lord, a face brightens upon understanding a new truth—these stories need to be shared. Volunteers rejoice upon hearing the results of others' efforts in the classroom. And, as they gather for training, they will be inspired to share their own stories.

These stories, combined with Scripture and other things you choose to share at the meeting, can provide tremendous encouragement to your workers. The training meeting is your chance to come to the rescue with a dose of spiritual renewal. I'm confident you will see morale hit new heights when you begin to hold regular teacher training!

## Providing Social Time

In most churches those who teach in Sunday school or children's church are giving up an adult Sunday school class of their own to be with the children. The volunteer who makes this sacrifice should be given other opportunities for fellowship with other believers. Teacher training can provide this in various ways. Depending on the structure of your meeting, it will provide a time to laugh, relax, and get to know others on a more personal level.

At some point during your meeting you may want to use a get-acquainted game, or have volunteers share brief personal testimonies, giving everyone the opportunity to know more about each other. Small buzz groups during the refreshment time provide the chance to share with each other facts about family and work life. Your meetings can help volunteers make friends with others in the church body. At some meetings they will simply enjoy having a few moments, without structure, in order to fellowship with each other.

## Equipping Volunteers

It's essential to equip your volunteers to understand children and to learn proper teaching techniques. If you do not properly train your volunteers, you will most likely lose them. Some of the topics that a teacher or other children's worker may need training in include:

It's essential to equip your volunteers to understand children and to learn proper teaching techniques.

lesson preparation, using curriculum, age-level characteristics, different ways children learn, discipline techniques, leading a child to Christ, effective Bible use, building self-esteem in children, and motivating learners. What a responsibility you have been given!

Perhaps you don't feel adequate to train teachers because you have come into this position as a volunteer yourself. Or perhaps you are still working toward the goal of adequately staffing your church with children's workers. You might think, "How can I focus on training? I have enough trouble convincing people to show up to teach the class." Don't lose heart—there are still ways for you to properly equip your children's ministry staff. Your workers need confidence that they can do the job, and they will only feel that way if you are also confident that God will equip you to do *your* job. It is my sincere wish that as you go through this manual you will gain valuable insights on how to properly train your volunteers to do the very best job possible!

Let me suggest four absolutes that will keep your volunteers on board once they have begun teaching—

*Training:* Proper training gives volunteers the tools they need to do their jobs.

*Curriculum:* Good curriculum frees volunteers to develop their teaching techniques to full potential.

*Team teaching/Partnership:* Having someone available to provide support, encouragement, and problem-solving will give your volunteers confidence and enthusiasm for their ministry. Assigning every volunteer a team teacher, no matter how small the class, will also help give hm or her a sense of having a ministry partner.

*Prayer:* Regular prayer entrusts your volunteers to God's care and affirms the truth that the results of your efforts are ultimately in His hands.

If you lack any of these four, you will no doubt burn out your workers and they will go down in defeat. That's why I'm offering you some significant ways to administer effective teacher training in the pages ahead! But before you go on, take a minute to complete the following exercises.

# Taking the next step:

Write your overall philosophy of children's ministry. (For additional help in developing a philosophy of children's ministry, consult *The Recruiting Remedy*, published by David C. Cook.)

_____

_____

_____

_____

_____

_____

_____

List and describe in your own words at least five benefits of teacher training to yourself and your volunteers:

1._____

_____

2._____

_____

3._____

_____

4._____

_____

5._____

_____

Three objections to regular teacher training you might hear, and how you'd respond to them:

**Objection:**_____

_____

**Response:**_____

_____

**Objection:**_____

_____

**Response:**_____

_____

**Objection:**_____

_____

**Response:**_____

_____

# DETERMINE
## your approach to teacher training

*"We'll have the best trained teachers in the conference!"*

### When you have taken this step, you will be able to:

● Identify and implement the ideal structure for teacher training.
● Develop plans for monthly or quarterly meetings, and/or annual retreats.
● State three reasons why regular training is essential for successful children's ministry.

# Making Teacher Training Work in Your Church

When I think of the volunteers that work with the children in our churches—the future leaders of Christ's church—I think of them as pivotal people in the building up of young saints. But who is going to build up *the builders?*

I realized that if I were ever going to learn to ski successfully I would need a trainer—someone I trusted, who understood my fears of inadequacy. And one lesson a year wouldn't be enough. I would need lessons pretty often for me to build up my self-confidence and be able to go it alone on the slopes. I was very busy, however, and I thought that a weekly lesson would be a little hard to fit into my schedule. Would I be willing to give up one Saturday a month to learn to ski? Maybe, but I would have to see progress and I would have to feel it was really worth it.

Many volunteers feel the same way about teacher training. It seems almost impossible to give up another night of the week, or every Saturday morning. But if you reason with them, helping them see the value to themselves and to their students, you will likely get a commitment to at least one training session per month. In light of the benefits, they should be willing to make that sacrifice.

## Make Training Regular

If you you have not determined in your own mind that REGULAR training is necessary, then you will probably have a hard time making it a successful endeavor. Here's why regular training is so essential . . .

*Training reduces teacher turnover.* It's true! Teacher training makes a significant difference in the length of time your volunteers will serve. As they begin to see the quality of their teaching improve, their confidence and enthusiasm for the task will grow. As they begin to feel really cared for and nurtured, they will be on the road to some very effective ministry. But this situation takes time to build. It will take many months before you reap such rewards for your efforts.

Basically, we need to see recruitment and training as intertwined. Our tendency is to believe that once we have recruited volunteers and placed them in a classroom they will be there until the end of time. Unfortunately, that attitude is the reason more people do not come forward to teach. They envision being thrown into a classroom with a teacher's manual, some crayons, and a rope to tie up the kids long enough to make them listen. And they see you locking the door and throwing away the key!

*Good, consistent communication helps keep volunteers committed and gives them the encouragement they need . . .*

Because we spend so much time coaxing volunteers into the classroom, we forget that the responsibility of recruitment does not end when they begin teaching. The Sunday your volunteer begins teaching is the same Sunday you take on the responsibility of continuing his or her "recruitment" through regular training.

*Training fulfills the call to disciple others.* Since placing volunteers in the classroom is only the initial step to recruiting them, you must now give them the confidence and the desire to continue in their ministry to children. This is called discipleship. Teacher training is a big part of discipling volunteers.

Psalm 78:72 talks about David's leadership of those under his care: "And David shepherded [fed] them with integrity of heart; with skillful hands he led them." Lorne Sanny, of the Navigators, says about this verse: "In that one statement we find the functions, qualities, and tools of leadership. The functions of leadership are to feed and to guide. You feed the person and guide them in their task. The qualities of leadership are character and competence, the person and the task. The tools of leadership are heart and hand, a heart for the people and a helping hand for the task." There can be no greater helping hand to your volunteers than regular training.

*Training gives crucial help.* It takes much tenacity to get your volunteers to believe that teacher training will benefit them in ways they never dreamed possible. "Do we have to have another meeting? I'm all meetinged out," they say. Yet you can see a dramatic change in that attitude after a volunteer participates in a meeting that is well-structured and filled with real "meat"—practical information and training—for them to sink their teeth into. No one has the time to come to a meeting to discuss how much PlayDoh is in Room 2. Yet, when meetings prove to be vital to effective teaching, your volunteers will start looking forward to them.

The volunteer who says, "I don't need any training; I've taught Sunday school for years," will need to be given the broader picture. This is the volunteer who needs to know the philosophy of your ministry and what goals you are trying to achieve. Also, he or she may need to see the development of "team spirit" as the significant reason for attending.

Whatever approach you take, it is important for you to begin now to make teacher training a regular part of your Christian education program.

*Because teachers often miss their own Sunday school classes or worship services, their spiritual tanks can start to run dry.*

## Communicate the Vision

Good, consistent communication helps keep volunteers committed and gives them the encouragement they need for ongoing ministry with children. And you can communicate most effectively by gathering people together in a group. Why? If you try to relay a message, a vision, or a value to your volunteers individually, you will be relaying a somewhat different message to each person. The process then becomes like the "telephone" game we used to play around the table: One person begins whispering a message to the next, and by the time it gets to the last person, it's a completely different message! On the other hand, if you have your audience together as a group, you can impart your goals and visions to everyone at the same time with clarity and impact. This also gives them the opportunity to ask any questions, to clarify anything they may have misunderstood. Having them together in a group gives them a feeling of ownership of their ministry, especially as you give them the opportunity to ask questions and to make suggestions for changes within the ministry.

Your communication style will make a big difference in how your volunteers respond to you. For example, if you approach your precious volunteers with an attitude of apology for having a meeting, the meetings will not be too successful. Your strong, confident attitude and determination to help them succeed will make all the difference in the world.

Expect great things! Even before you approach the subject of teacher training with your volunteers, be ready with your own plans and preparations. Your expectation level will be met most of the time. If you expect nothing you will likely get nothing. I've found that when I've expected more from my volunteers, I've gotten more. Others will sense the extreme importance you place on teacher training and they will be inspired to make it a priority in their own lives.

## Provide the Orientation

At the beginning of the year, your volunteers will need a time of orientation. This can be done in a teacher training session. Each volunteer needs to know a number of things at the outset: how to find their way around the church campus, how to order supplies, how to obtain curriculum, and how to deal with various other problems that will arise. A basic training class might be offered to each new volunteer coming into the children's ministry. You will find suggestions later in this manual on the subjects to be covered.

*". . . The tools of leadership are heart and hand, a heart for the people and a helping hand for the task."*

## Use Written Resources

A vast amount of excellent reading material is available for us today. Use it in your work with volunteers. For example, you could set up a Children s Ministry Library, or Ministry Resource Center for your teachers. Books on every aspect of childhood development, from discipline to building children's self-esteem, will provide the expertise your volunteers need to excel in children's ministry.

## Aim for the Ideal

The ideal structure for teacher training is to hold a monthly meeting, the perfect opportunity for every department to come together to plan for the coming month. This arrangement gives each department a chance to discuss problems and make decisions regarding assignments of tasks for the month (for example, who will lead singing, provide crafts, plan pre-session activities, etc.). **Resources 1 and 2** will help volunteers with their planning for each Sunday.

These classroom planner sheets will greatly help the new teacher or any substitute helpers you may have in your classroom. The planner sheet assigns each person in the room the task they will be doing for that morning or for the month. Fill in the time column with the schedule for the morning: what time you will arrive, what time each thing on the schedule is happening. As each teacher, helper, or substitute enters the room he or she can glance at this planner to determine what ministry area to be in throughout the entire morning.

If you have a large class, you may find this sheet helpful in dividing the children into color groups so that you may rotate them for the story, craft, playground use or any other crowded space that you have. Putting colored name tags on the children to correspond with their group assignment will help the pre-schooler to identify his or her group immediately. Notice on the sample chart when each group rotates in and out of each activity. This is very helpful when your classrooms are over-crowded.

Not only will monthly meetings initiate good planning, they will reduce the workload of recruiting. As volunteers become proficient at what they are doing they will become more and more comfortable and, thus, stay with teaching a lot longer.

So, monthly training is the ideal and should be your goal as you go forward in your ministry. However, if you are a layperson, a Sunday school superintendent, or even a part-time children's director, it may be a real sacrifice for you to plan and execute a monthly training session.

If monthly training seems overwhelming to you because of other time commitments, consider alternative ways to meet your training needs.

## Consider the Alternatives

If monthly training seems overwhelming to you because of other time commitments, consider alternative ways to meet your training needs.

*Schedule quarterly meetings.* During the first year you could plan to hold quarterly training. This is an ideal way to begin to interest your volunteers in regular teacher training. But if you use quarterly training, do it with excellence! These times together should warmly convey to each participant: "You are very special and so is this time we are going to spend together."

Quarterly meetings may need to be a little longer in length, perhaps covering an entire Saturday morning, but you could use a schedule similar to that of a monthly meeting. All of the steps we will be discussing in the chapters ahead can be used in whatever training calendar you decide to adopt.

Your quarterly meetings could have holiday themes. For example, you could hold your first meeting in October using fall colors and decorations, fall leaf or pumpkin name tags, with "The Teacher as a Role Model" for your emphasis. Then begin the New Year with a second meeting based on a New Year's Party theme. Your training subject could be

"Discipline" or "Guided Conversation." Your April meeting would relate to Easter or spring, with pastel-egg name tags and Easter baskets for decor. Spend some time giving Easter ideas for the classroom, plus teaching your group a few children's songs for Easter. In July or August your meeting could use ice cream as a theme, and focus on planning for the beginning of the new year of Christian education.

*Plan annual retreats.* If you have never offered teacher training, or you want to do something a lot different, you could plan a Children's Ministry Retreat. It could cover a Friday evening and all day Saturday at the church. A special speaker or trainer could be brought in to do the training.

Another way to do a retreat is to plan an entire weekend dedicated to children's ministry—away from the church at a rented campground or retreat center. (Of course, a distant retreat would require substitutes in each classroom on Sunday morning. Yet, this could be a perfect opportunity for a congregation and parents to show its children's team how much they appreciate their hard work—by filling in for them one Sunday a year!)

A weekend away in a camp setting,

*A weekend away in a camp setting, or even at a hotel, is an ideal way to get the undivided attention of your children's volunteers.*

or even at a hotel, is an ideal way to get the undivided attention of your children's volunteers. Participating in a series of practical workshops, and experiencing extended fellowship with others in the same ministry, will give them a burst of energy for the rest of the year.

Your retreat schedule should provide plenty of time for volunteers to get acquainted with one another. Include some games and fun activities, and structure times of significant sharing together. On Sunday mornings or during the midweek program it is usually impossible for people to see the other departments and to know who is working with them to build up the children of the church. But at the retreat they can rub shoulders with the others in their area of ministry, and be mutually encouraged.

Give the volunteers an opportunity to share the thrill of victory with one another. Ask them to tell about children responding to the Gospel, changing their attitudes, changing their behaviors, receiving answers to their prayers. People ministering to children often do not see the fruit of their labors for many years. So it's exciting to hear about the children that are responding!

Because teachers often miss their own Sunday school classes or worship services, their spiritual tanks can start to run dry. A special spiritual emphasis at the retreat will help them regain spiritual energy. Consider having a guest speaker who can encourage and inspire tired or frustrated workers. Teaching children is a sacrificial ministry. So, try to keep your volunteers spiritually fed and feeling loved. A retreat can be just what the doctor ordered to enlighten and inspire those special people who minister to the children of your church.

# Taking the next step:

How might the following structures for teacher training take shape in your church situation? Jot some notes in the spaces below.

**REGULAR MONTHLY TRAINING MEETINGS**

Advantages: _____

_____

_____

Potential problems/solutions: _____

_____

_____

**ALTERNATIVE: QUARTERLY TRAINING MEETINGS**

Advantages: _____

_____

_____

Potential problems/solutions: _____

_____

_____

**ALTERNATIVE: ANNUAL RETREAT**

Advantages: _____

_____

_____

Potential problems/solutions: _____

_____

_____

Pick the one structure that seems best to start with. Make a list of the first three steps you would need to take to implement this form of training:

1. _____

2. _____

3. _____

# PLAN
## the training year

PORTLOCK

*"Hmm. Maybe we shouldn't schedule 'You can discipline Junior Highers' for April first, after all."*

## When you have taken this step, you will be able to:

- Assess your teachers' training needs.
- Develop basic and advanced topics for your training year.
- Plan a whole year of teacher training meetings.

# Looking Ahead to a Great Year of Teacher Training

**B**efore you can begin planning your training year, you will, of course, have to convince others that teacher training really is worthy of significant time and effort. How do you do that?

## Start Talking about Teacher Training

Begin to share your desire to hold regular, consistent meetings for the training of teachers. Let interested people know the reasons you feel this would be so valuable for the entire children's ministry.

*Expect some resistance.* Undoubtedly you will meet some resistance from some of your veteran teachers. Regrettably, those who have been teaching the longest may resist most firmly your push for regular training.

Yet, you can begin to share your heart with the teachers who are already teaching. Perhaps they need to better understand the practical value of teacher training. Take the opportunity to talk with volunteers about holding regular training as you are discussing problem areas with them. Or just mention some of your ideas in casual conversation with them. Soon they'll discover your pure motives for wanting to see growth in

their lives and in the lives of the children they are ministering to. And they will very likely catch the spirit of your vision for the Children's Team to be properly trained.

*Write it up, and hand it out.* The five reasons (given in chapter one) for holding training meetings could be typed up on cute cards, or presented in a special flyer (see **Resource 3**). Volunteers could hand these to parents and others who inquire about the purpose of children's ministry. Department leaders could use the handouts to orient new teachers to their departments while conveying a clear rationale for teacher training. Actually, any new people you recruit would benefit from such a written piece. It would let them know, before they begin, that teacher training is a normal part of their commitment to the children.

## Pick a Time—and Stick to It

Once you get the support you need to start regular teacher training, you must pick an appropriate time to begin your program. Use a natural break in the calendar, like the beginning of the new church year in September. But if you are reading this in November don't wait until next fall to begin. Start right after the holidays are over. A New Year's

> Meetings should be scheduled on
> a night when you can and will
> give it your very best time and
> effort.

resolution to have solid training would be great! Begin now. You can't begin too soon.

What's the best time to hold your regular meetings? You'll want to give this crucial question much thought and prayerful consideration.

*Get the night right.* Common sense tells you to pick a night that would be acceptable to the majority of the volunteers. So, as you approach your decision, you'll need to keep in mind the various local events, national holidays, school programs, and other days that may affect attendance at your training meetings. Yet, you need to begin somewhere. After considering all the factors mentioned, pick a night of the month that would fit nicely into the church calendar.

Warning: Don't ask for a vote from your volunteers to choose the best night. You will never meet everyone's needs. A vote will only create instant feelings of resentment if you don't meet on the particular night someone voted for. Therefore, the decision should be yours.

Meetings should be scheduled on a night when *you* can and will give it your very best time and effort. Clear the night with the rest of the church staff and then immediately put it in place on the church calendar. It is always of utmost impor-

tance to have the night as free from other church activities as possible.

*Take another look at Sunday.*
Though evening meetings seem to be the best way to accommodate peoples' work schedules, an alternative would be to hold your training meetings about every third month on a Sunday morning—as impossible as that seems! Obtain substitute teachers for every class, asking parents and others to fill in for this one Sunday so the regular teachers may be free to attend teacher training. Then begin early with a continental breakfast and launch into your meeting.

The success of this approach will depend largely on your church size and your morning worship schedule. It has been used quite successfully in some churches I have visited. Your meeting time might be shortened considerably, however.

Another occasional alternative would be a Saturday morning meeting. Most of us do not like to give up our weekends, particularly if we are working during the week. However, a Saturday morning meeting once in a while might be a change from another night meeting. Quarterly meetings would work well on a Saturday, from 9-12. This would automatically extend your meeting time, giving you more time than a typical evening meeting.

As a rule, you should only change the meeting
night for things as important
as national holidays.

*Be consistent.* Always schedule the meetings on the same night of the month. Don't waiver when a person calls in and asks if it couldn't be changed—just this once. As a rule, you should only change the meeting night for things as important as national holidays. (For example, if you schedule your meetings on the fourth Thursday of every month, you will have a hard time in November, since your meeting would fall on Thanksgiving. Don't let that keep you from using the fourth Thursday of the month, if that is the best night for you. You simply move the meeting to the third Thursday in November.)

Remember, once you begin to make exceptions for individuals you will be asked constantly to make changes. But it isn't fair to the rest of the Children's Ministry Team to change the meeting night for one or two people. Your team should have the yearly calendar given to them at the beginning of the school year so there will be no excuse for anyone saying "I didn't know when the meeting was this month." We are creatures of habit. When your volunteers get tuned into the fourth Thursday or the second Tuesday that is when they will be ready for a meeting.

Of course, some volunteers will have conflicting work obligations. Or some college students may have classes in the evening. These situations would provide valid excuses for not attending a meeting. (I would not put such persons in place as department leaders since it will be vitally important for your department heads to be at your monthly meetings.) So, while you encourage regular attendance, remember that your volunteers are often faced with real scheduling challenges. My policy was to say that those who were working, attending classes in the evening, or ill, had valid reasons for missing a meeting.

## Assess Your Teachers' Needs

You should be able to determine better than any other person what the training needs of your teachers are. If they have never been given any training at all, you will probably need to begin with the basics.

*Start with basic topics.* Make a list of the subjects or skills you sense your teachers need help with the most. Then prioritize them to see where you want to start. Certain subject areas and skills would be considered basic requirements for all teachers, while some would be necessary for anyone working with children.

The ideal situation would be to develop a pre-service Basic Training Class that volunteers could take prior to

You should be able to determine better
than any other person what the training
needs of your teachers are.

actually teaching in a classroom. It could be taught for six weeks, once a week. However, in most situations volunteers would be placed in a classroom prior to finishing Basic Training, because of the great need for teachers. If they do take the class simultaneously with teaching, be sure they would continue on with in-service training.

Subjects to consider for Basic Training would be:
• Leading a Child to Christ
• How to Plan a Lesson/Use Curriculum
• How to Schedule the Teaching Hour
• Classroom Discipline
• Age-Level Characteristics: How Students Learn
• Storytelling
• Guided Conversation

*Move to advanced topics.* Once you feel your teachers are quite strong in the basic areas you may want to schedule more advanced training. There really is no end to what can be covered in teacher training meetings. Be creative! Let me give you a list to start with—

• The Teacher as Role Model
• Becoming Part of the Student's Life Outside the Classroom

• Classroom Decor/Bulletin Boards
• The Teacher's Prayer Life
• Resources for Teaching
• Easter Activities for the Classroom
• Christmas Activities for the Classroom
• Music for the Musically Improving Teacher
• Bible-Learning Activities
• Great Pre-session Activities
• Building the Child's Self-Esteem
• Using Learning Centers
• Building Staff Relationships
• Effective Home Visitation
• How to Develop and Ask Effective Questions
• Learning Styles: How to Make the Most of Them

## Plan for the Whole Year

A monthly planning calendar will enable you to see, at a glance, what you will be doing throughout the entire year (see **Resources 4 and 5**). Resource 4 will give you some ideas on how to plan your monthly calendar. This gives a guideline for some of the things that can be done in planning the entire year in advance. Events other than teacher training are mentioned if they would involve the whole Children's Ministry Team. Resource 5 is a blank calendar for you to fill in as you best see fit. Begin by penciling in each month's topic. Then—

Rather than having a regular meeting
in December, for instance, you might choose to
host an open house at your home.

*Schedule the meetings.* In some parts of the country you would not schedule meetings during the summer vacation months. Or perhaps you would skip June and July but have a meeting in August to gear up for September. Usually training meetings would not be scheduled in December. Be consistent, but be flexible, too.

And be creative as you prepare your yearly planning calendar. Use clip art to embellish it and show that you have clearly planned the whole year. You should begin planning the calendar two months ahead of your scheduled beginning, so that you will be completely prepared to hand your calendar to each volunteer at your kick-off meeting. Your staff will see your deep dedication to their training just by observing the time and effort you have put into your planning calendar.

Some planning decisions you make will be based on your geographic location as well as the church calendar. For example, many cities have begun year-round school, thus changing the times we might promote "release time."

You must keep seasonal factors in mind as well. Rather than having a regular meeting in December, for instance, you might choose to host an open house at your home. Most volunteers will enjoy being given a special treat during the holiday season. Others will appreciate the option of missing a meeting during the busy holiday month.

Whether to schedule meetings during summer break will be your own personal decision. Even though they have committed to a year of teaching, people do need to take vacations. They need to have the freedom to be gone for two or three weeks during the summer months. You may decide that it's best not to hold teacher training during these months.

*Think through the activities.* Once your calendar is full, begin to consider what you will do in each of the meetings. Do you want to bring in an outside speaker for some of them? Would a film cover the subject you've chosen on a particular night? How about having some of the teachers do skits to illustrate the topic in a humorous way?

Within your own volunteer staff there will be people you may use as resources. Observe how your volunteers minister. You will see that some are strong in Bible-learning activities or in setting up learning centers. Others will have special strengths in discipline, planning the teaching hour, or greeting the children. So consider occasionally asking one of your own teachers—someone the other teachers would respect—to take the teaching portion of a meeting.

No matter how trained a volunteer may feel, he or she needs to become part of a team and to catch a vision for the entire program of children's ministry in your church.

## Use Good Training Materials

If you have never planned or led a teacher training meeting, I want to let you know that there is nothing to fear. You can do it! I felt like the greenest recruit on the face of the earth when I began my career as Children's Director. I did not have a clue where to begin, but I did know that God had placed me in my position and He would be faithful to me there. He was, and He will be for you.

You may have public school teachers, perhaps even a college professor, doctors, lawyers, and other professionals in your volunteer staff. Don't let that inhibit you. Remember your five reasons for teacher training: to impart your vision for the ministry, build a team spirit, offer encouragement, provide a social time, and equip your volunteers with technique training. Every volunteer, no matter how qualified in other areas, can benefit from these aspects of teacher training. No matter how trained a volunteer may feel, he or she needs to become part of a team and to catch a vision for the entire program of children's ministry in your church.

Your success will depend largely on your ability to offer very practical help in each and every meeting. Thus, you will need to find and use the best training materials available. How do you find them? Here are some ideas:

*Talk to others in children's ministry.*
Begin talking to other children's ministry people. Ask them what materials they have used and what ideas they might have for teacher training topics. Most children's workers are eager to share their ideas so that others' ministries will grow and children (and their leaders) will be spiritually enriched.

If there is no children's ministry group holding regular meetings in your area, take the initiative to form one. Send invitations to the workers in churches in your area that you feel would be interested in meeting once a month for lunch. If just two or three of you meet you will have a significant forum for sharing ideas and vision. Great encouragement comes from shared experiences. You may be able to visit others' teacher training meetings to glean ideas and gain insight into what you yourself would like to see accomplished at your own meetings.

*Visit your local Christian bookstore.*
Go to your local Christian book store and plan to spend several hours looking through the available teacher training materials. Talk with the Christian Education Department manager to ask questions and receive any information on new materials or those that will be coming out soon. While you are there

> Create an atmosphere that would
> make you feel good about your teaching if you
> were one of your volunteers.

you may wish to make an appointment to preview films or videos you could use in teacher training. One book from David C. Cook called *Ready-to-Use Teacher Training Sessions*, by Ellen Larson is ideally suited for use in regular training meetings.

 *Attend Sunday school conventions.*
If you live in an area where there is no Christian bookstore, make every effort to attend state or regional Sunday School conventions. You'll be able to attend workshops related to all areas of children's ministry. And you'll find numerous resources to review at these conferences. While attending a convention you should ask to be placed on the mailing list of all publishers represented. Once you are on their mailing lists you will receive current catalogs as well as samples of curriculum and other materials.

 *Check local Christian college and seminary libraries.* If you are fortunate enough to live near a Christian college or seminary, visit its library to see what CE materials are available. Perhaps a faculty member or a graduate student interested in CE could assist you in some way.

## Loose Your Creativity!

My teenage son once encouraged me with some words that have become a motto for me as I work in children's ministry. He said: "Let your juices flow Mom; be creative. Just relax and *let your creative juices flow.*"

You have creative juices, too. Let them flow! Think big thoughts about your teacher training. Create an atmosphere that would make you feel good about your teaching if you were one of your volunteers. You are the host or hostess for every meeting. When company comes to your home, you want it to be the very nicest you can make it. It is no different for your volunteers. Each meeting should be a mini "thank you" for all their labors of love.

# Taking the next step:

My teachers' greatest training needs are:

_____
_____
_____
_____
_____

Some basic topics to be covered in training meetings:

_____
_____
_____
_____
_____

Some advanced topics to be considered for training meetings:

_____
_____
_____
_____
_____

My plans for finding the best materials include checking with the following persons and places:

_____
_____
_____
_____
_____

If you have not done so already, fill in **Resource 5** with your plans for the training year.

# PREPARE
## your first meeting

*"Got it? Anybody tries to run for the exits, you tackle 'em."*

## When you have taken this step, you will be able to:

- Plan the schedule and the activities for your first meeting.
- Identify and use various involvement methods in your first meeting.
- Use a checklist to prepare the details for your first meeting.
- Design an attractive flyer to advertise your first meeting.

# Getting Everything Ready for Your First Training Event

If you have not completed your yearly planning calendar for teacher training, do so before you continue with your planning. Make decisions regarding the times, dates, and training subjects you will be covering in the coming year. Once the yearly calendar is complete it will be time to plan your first individual meeting.

## Prepare with Purpose

*Schedule your session time.* You will want to plan the time schedule and how you envision the meeting flowing. (See the suggested schedule in **Resource 6**. The difference between the two plans is to reverse your technique training and your departmental planning time. If you choose to have your departmental planning time at the beginning of your meeting, be prepared for people to stay too long in their planning sessions and not get back on time for the technique training. The ideal way seems to be Plan A. If the departmental planning gets long, they have the extra time to spend at the close of the evening, rather than miss the heart of the meeting.) Plan not only the topics for each meeting but the "trimmings" that will add sparkle to your meetings as well. (**Resource 7** will help you with this.) The extra little touches that you add to the

meetings show your volunteers how valuable they are to you. It will take considerable organizing time to prepare fully for each meeting.

*Outline your lesson activities.* Outline your technique training lesson. The outline will likely fall into place as you review all the materials you will be using. You may want to use resources from many places. If you find one lesson outline for teaching a particular subject, yet you have learned ideas from other places, by all means incorporate those ideas. It is okay to combine all your resources. Consider these two basic approaches to the use of materials:

• You may choose to use a pre-prepared teacher training lesson. This can be very beneficial if you are just beginning as a trainer. Such training materials will usually give you the time schedule, pre-session ideas, list of things needed, room set-up suggestions, handouts for your teaching time, and pages you can reproduce as overheads. All the planning work for the actual training presentation has been done for you. Yet, if you are new to teacher training, even these pre-prepared lessons can seem overwhelming. If there seems to be too much material in any one session simply use only what best fits your needs. Pick and choose those activities that are most

*Someone who is actively involved in the learning process will be much more encouraged and motivated than one who sits inactive throughout a meeting.*

suitable to you.

One sample lesson to get you started can be found on page 57. As mentioned earlier, *Ready-to-Use Teacher Training Sessions* by Ellen Larson (David C. Cook) is an excellent source of meeting plans.

• You may choose to use your own self-developed materials. If you feel more confident using your own material, then use it and let your enthusiasm for imparting your personal knowledge and experience flow through to the participants. Whatever material you decide to use, you will feel most confident when you have it outlined and know the material well. So do plan to study your material and have full command of it.

## Include Involvement

By all means use high-involvement methods in your meetings. Someone who is actively involved in the learning process will be much more encouraged and motivated than one who sits inactive throughout a meeting.

A recent Bell and Howell study clearly showed that we retain 10% of what we read, 20% of what we hear, 30% of what we see, 40% of what we hear and see, 70% of what we say and 90% of what we *say and do*. Students need to be actively involved in a learning experience as much as possible. At your teacher training meetings, your volunteers are suddenly the students and not the teachers!

*Be sensitive to learning styles.*
People learn in different ways. At any given meeting there will be people who absorb the material presented in different ways. They have different learning styles. It will benefit your volunteers to become aware of the different learning styles and understand how to vary teaching methods so that all students learn at their maximum level. According to Bernice McCarthy (*The 4Mat System: Teaching to Learning Styles with Right-Left Mode Techniques*, Excel Publications, Barrington IL, 1980), there are four basic learning styles: Imaginative Learners, Analytic Learners, Common Sense Learners, and Dynamic Learners.

•Imaginative Learners study life as it is lived. They perceive events around them and generalize. They evaluate a learning experience as a whole rather than trying to break it down into parts. It is more important for an Imaginative Learner to get along with other people than to be right. This learner learns by listening and sharing.

•Analytic Learners are thinkers and watchers. They are rational and sequential in their thinking patterns. They do not make snap decisions. They are usu-

> Always try to model for your volunteers
> everything you want them to do
> with their students in the classroom.

ally the people who excel in school situations. They prefer decoding written, verbal, and image symbols over working with people.

•Common Sense Learners start with an idea, try it out, conduct experiments, and test it. They thrive in situations that offer hands-on experience. They value strategic thinking and are skills-oriented. They want to know the personal benefits of a learning situation before launching into it.

•Dynamic Learners see, hear, touch, feel, and then plunge into something and try it out for themselves. They have experimental attitudes and accompanying behaviors. They work to make things better. They excel in situations calling for flexibility.

 *Use a variety of methods and activities.* Using methods that appeal to all four learning styles will keep everyone's interest at a high level. You may not be able to cater to all four learning styles at every meeting, but at least vary your meetings so everyone will be able to relate to his or her learning style at some of the meetings. Here are some examples of varieties of methods and activities you could try:

*Pre-session activities.* These are a must. Pre-session activities get

your volunteers right into the theme for the evening. Have something prepared for getting participants involved the moment they arrive. You may want to have your instructions on the overhead projector so that as people straggle in you will not have to repeat yourself. For example, an evening on building self-esteem may begin with participants folding a paper clip to demonstrate one thing they feel has enhanced their own self-esteem. Or plan some uncomplicated get-acquainted games for an effective pre-session. Most published teacher training sessions include suggestions for pre-session activities.

*Modeling.* Always try to model for your volunteers everything you want them to do with their students in the classroom. If you ask them to be in their classrooms fifteen minutes before class, then you should be at teacher training fifteen minutes early! If learning begins the moment a child enters the room, it is no different for your teachers.

*Visual aids.* Visual aids involve your teachers without calling on them to put forth much effort. Subconsciously, people learn just by what is placed on the wall in a room. Large posters made from butcher paper with key words written on them in bright

Always preview any film or video you are
planning to use in training.

colors would immediately key your participants into learning as they enter the room. Or you could string a clothesline across the room and hang on it some large squares of paper (with clothespins) presenting the important issues of the evening's topic. Whatever the theme you pick for your meeting, decorate your meeting room accordingly.

*Buzz groups.* It helps any learner to be involved rather than just listen to someone talk about a particular subject. You may want to give a short lecture on guided conversation, then create questions to be used in buzz groups for a discussion time. Follow up group discussion by having each group share a summary of its discoveries.

*Films or videos.* Showing a film may not seem like a way to involve your volunteers in the meeting! Yet, you can powerfully drive home a point through a film or video presentation. Once you have shown the film you could assemble participants in small groups and ask them to work on answering questions you have written about the film. Most people want to talk about any movie they have just watched, and with stimulating questions they will become very involved. Note: Always preview any film or video you are planning to

use in training. You will want to be in complete agreement with all the ideas presented before you show the production to others. Three films I recommend are "The Stray," "He Leadeth Me," and "Cipher in the Snow."

*Skits.* These are both fun and challenging. Skits can be done as elaborately or as simply as you wish. For example, you may be having a meeting on "How to Conduct Effective Home Visitation." Construct a home's front door out of a refrigerator carton, or set up a mock living room. Ask a group to demonstrate the proper way to visit and then another group could demonstrate some improper ways to call on their students. Most people love to ham it up, and principles conveyed in skit form are rarely forgotten!

*Music.* A theme like: "Music in the Sunday School for the Musically Improving Teacher" can bring out the best in even the most non-musical teachers. Most will enjoy learning how to use a harmonica, autoharp, or other simple instrument. Involve them in singing songs they will be teaching to their classes, using body and finger motions. You'll find warmth and laughter flowing as teachers gain the expertise they so desperately need to keep their class-

Any method that gets your teaching staff
actively involved in the meeting
to make it theirs—use it!

rooms inviting and lively. (If you are not musically inclined, recruit a musical person to conduct the musical portion of the meeting.)

*Live demonstrations.* Bringing children into the classroom for a live demonstration of how to apply certain techniques is a nice change for your volunteers as well as for you. Perhaps one of your teachers does an excellent job with guided conversation or storytelling. Ask him or her to demonstrate that expertise with some of the Sunday school children.

Any method that gets your teaching staff actively involved in the meeting to make it theirs—use it!

## Look at a List

To successfully integrate regular teacher training into your church program, you must proceed with good planning and organization. And you will be more relaxed and able to minister to your volunteers when you have the added confidence that comes with being well prepared. So consider using checklists for everything you plan.

Working through a checklist keeps you from forgetting important details (see **Resource 8**). It helps you on the day of the meeting, as well as ahead of time, to know what you will need to order or purchase. Here's how a good checklist could help you prepare:

*Supplies.* Order and purchase all supplies. Different parts of the meeting may require purchases or assembling of supplies. You may want to find a volunteer to help you with these kinds of errands. There are probably a number of people in your congregation who prefer *not* to work directly with children but who *do* want to be of service in other areas of children's ministry.

*Name Tags.* If you are serving in a large church, name tags can help you remember the names of volunteers until you get to know each one personally. But it is equally important for volunteers in different areas of service to know the names of those serving with them on the Children's Ministry Team. Since one of your primary goals is to build a team spirit, you will want everyone to know each others' names and areas of ministry. If you involve your midweek volunteers in the same training session with Sunday morning workers, you might have different types of name tags for each group. (See **Resource 9** for samples of name tags.) Be sure pens are available for writing on the name tags.

Holiday name tags are fun for special times of the year (see **Resource 10**). Any-

You will be more relaxed and able to minister
to your volunteers when you have the added
confidence that comes with being well prepared.

thing you can do to make your first meeting a special event will give the message to your volunteers that you value them.

✓ *Icebreakers*. These activities help group members relax and get to know one another. Since your volunteers are people who love children, they are likely the "fun-loving types." Plan the activities you will use for getting acquainted (see **Resources 11 and 12**). Plan some icebreakers just for the atmosphere of fun they create.

✓ *Refreshments.*There are two places you may want to use refreshments. First, you could provide an immediate snack. It was always fun for my volunteers to come to the meeting and find a small snack awaiting them near the sign-in sheet. For example, I placed individual candy bars or individually wrapped candy in a basket or appropriate container (in a pumpkin for Thanksgiving, or ceramic bunny for Easter). The coffee, hot tea, iced tea, or cider was always ready when they arrived.

Second, you should provide refreshments for the meeting itself. These will be more substantial than just the little opening snack. But please—*DON'T have the volunteers bring the refreshments.* Remember, you are the host for this

event. Many of your volunteers work and will barely have the energy to come to the meeting without having to prepare their own refreshments.

If it is not in your budget to order donuts and cider, cake or pie, or a holiday-type treat (or a nice veggie tray, if you have dieters in your group), then I would suggest "congregational caterers." The senior citizens group, or perhaps the parents of the children, would probably be glad to volunteer to do this for the teachers once a month. I would recommend a universal recipe so that all the refreshments are the same. Something simple is usually the best. An elaborate  dessert is not necessary. Just something special enough to make participants feel the care you are giving.

You'll save time and energy by finding a "refreshment chairperson," someone to be responsible to see that the refreshments are prepared ahead of time by calling the volunteers for you. You could also arrange for a serving committee to be at the meeting to serve for you, freeing you up to minister and train the volunteers.

✓ *Audiovisual Equipment*. Depending on the size of your church, you will need to rent or reserve any required audiovisual equipment. Make any arrangements for obtaining the

Your creative room decorations will add
pizazz to your meetings.

equipment well ahead of time. If you do not have your own church equipment, there are other options available to you. For example, you could start an "audiovisual pool" with other children's ministries in your area. Renting from local audiovisual agencies is also an alternative.

✓ *Decorations.* Your creative room decorations will add pizazz to your meetings. During certain holiday times or special events you may want to decorate your room as if you were having a party. Crepe paper streamers and helium balloons can add a real note of excitement.

Of course, you don't have to wait for a holiday to decorate. You can develop special times and themes of your own. For example, have a New Year's party in September, since it is the beginning of a new school year. Or throw a once-a-year birthday party for all the teachers.

At every meeting you will be using visual aids on your walls and across the room. A lesson on any subject is greatly enhanced by wall visuals or hand-held visuals. Work with some of your volunteers to paint large posters or special pictures that will contribute to the learning process. Large banners with the year's theme verse should be up at every meeting.

✓ *Prizes.* Purchase prizes to be given out for every reason you can think of—perfect attendance by individuals, classrooms, or clubs; a special missions project completed; any noteworthy accomplishment to be honored. This is a fun way to stimulate interest in the meeting.

Shop at discount stores for the little goodies that people love to receive. Buy things that are for their personal use, so they feel as if they have received a special treat from you. You may want to surprise the department directors with a little something extra occasionally if they called to remind their people of the meeting. There is no end to the creative ways you can use to help them know they are special people.

Give special certificates to individual volunteers for service above and beyond the call of duty (see **Resource 13**). Think of the many creative ways you could honor your volunteers. A Second-Miler button can be given at every meeting to the volunteer who has gone the second mile. This will take some investigating on your part and alertness to what is happening in and out of the classroom. All sorts of specialty buttons can be used for helping your volunteers feel special (see **Resource 14**).

> If your invitation is attractive, the meeting will be attractive. Boring flyers also send a message: boring meeting.

✓ *Games.* Don't forget to plan games for the social time. They need to be varied from month to month. Sometimes you will want to use get-acquainted games or quiet word games with not too much physical activity. At other meetings you may want to do a few more active games, like passing Lifesavers on toothpicks or tying a balloon on everyone's ankle and then seeing which team can break the balloons the fastest. Purchasing a game book will be a real boost to your own creativity. You'll find plenty of them at any bookstore.

## Forward a Flyer, Then Phone

You can design the notice for your meeting ahead of time so that you will be prepared to mail it at the appropriate time. Make the flyer colorful and full of life. Use catchy phrases with good pictures that represent the theme of the meeting. If your invitation is attractive, the meeting will be attractive. Boring flyers also send a message: boring meeting. **Resources 15 through 19** are examples of flyers for meetings.

If you don't own a clip art book, purchase one right away. If purchasing more books is not in your budget, a coloring book with cute children or animals can be a helpful alternative. (See **Resources 20 through 23 for** a clip art sample.) I can *think* of great looking

flyers and name tags, but the ability to put those ideas on paper is not one of my gifts. I could not survive without good clip art. A picture is worth a thousand words when we are enticing people to give up an evening to attend a meeting. You are in the process of showing them by the quality of your flyer how productive the meeting will be.

Include the time, place, room number, and the topic of the evening in your flyer. No long messages or explanations are necessary. People get bogged down with lots of verbiage. Just give the simple facts that are easily remembered.

Prepare the notice with great care, using correct grammar and spelling. Use rubber cement or printer's wax to glue clip art in place. A copy machine that will reduce your clip art to the size you need is available at most quick-copy centers.

If you have limited time, there are those in every church who enjoy art work. These people love to use their talents for the Lord and are waiting to be asked. Let them prepare the entire flyer for your approval, a good way for you to delegate some details that someone else would enjoy doing for you.

Mail the notice five days prior to the meeting. If you mail the notice too far ahead it won't serve its intended purpose to remind volunteers of the meet-

People get bogged down with lots of verbiage.
Just give the simple facts that
are easily remembered.

ing. Remember that each volunteer knows the meeting is scheduled for the same night of every month. The notice is simply a reminder that will also let them know the night's theme.

Telephone your key leaders two days prior to the meeting to remind them to telephone the people under them to attend the meeting. This is a great opportunity for you also to become better acquainted with your key leaders. It gives you the chance to have another means of communication with those very important people in your ministry.

*Cure for Teacher Training Insomnia: Counting Volunteers*

# Taking the next step:

The theme and/or topic for my first training meeting will be:

_____

The materials I will be using include:

_____

_____

_____

A rough outline for the teaching portion of the meeting might be:

_____

_____

_____

_____

_____

_____

_____

_____

_____

_____

_____

_____

_____

I will involve my volunteers with these interactive methods and activities:

_____

_____

_____

_____

I have completed the checklist found in Resource 8:  **YES   NO**

Here is a sketch of my flyer for the next meeting:

# HOLD
## your first meeting

*"No, you don't have the wrong room—this is the training meeting."*

### When you have taken this step, you will be able to:

- Cultivate an attitude of prayer and teachability.
- Review your plans for the first meeting.
- Prepare your room for the first meeting.
- Lead your first meeting, following a step-by-step process.
- Evaluate the results of your efforts.

# Starting off with Success

We are not here to initiate programs for God or His church. We are not to initiate anything. Our God has one great and burning passion upon His heart. It is to find a man here, another there, a woman here, another there and so fill them with His Holy Spirit that they may become channels through whom He can do what He plans to do." (Alan Redpath, *Victorious Christian Service*, Revell)

It's time to hold your first meeting. Are you nervous? The quote above should help calm your fears. It's an excellent reminder that all true ministry was first God's idea. And if His Spirit is motivating your ministry, it will be a success! So move ahead in faith, and in reliance upon His power.

## Lay the Groundwork

The person responsible for children's ministry, layperson or paid staff, has so many details to remember, so many programs to plan, so many people to recruit and train, that he or she may neglect the essential elements of all spiritual ministry—prayer and time in the Word.

*Have you prayed?* A key to the success of our entire ministry will be prayer. Yet it is so difficult to take the time to pray. Our lives are inundated with "good" things to do. The pressure of work, family life, ministry planning, meetings, getting the rooms in order for Sunday, and so much more cause us to give in to the immediate demands and forget the foundation. As we plan our training program for our volunteers, we must be willing to make time for prayer. So . . .

On the day of the meeting, in the morning, pray for God to move volunteers to attend that evening. Ask Him to work in the lives of those most likely not to attend. Ask Him to give them good work days with energy left over at the end of the day so they can be a part of a valuable growing time for them and their ministries.

Pray *very specifically* for your people. If this is your first meeting you will need to lift each one before the Lord. You perhaps know already the ones that are saying to you, "I don't need training," or "I don't have time for training meetings." Pray especially diligently for those volunteers.

*Do you have a teachable spirit?* Being teachable is one of the most mature character qualities a Christian can possess. But during your tenure as a children's ministry leader you will encounter those who are *not* teachable. In fact, many will feel they can teach you

*Being teachable is one of the most mature character qualities a Christian can possess.*

a few things about teaching children. Perhaps they can. Be open to learning from others.

I came into the job as Director of Children's Ministry by default and planned to stay in the position for three months until the church hired a "professional." But God had other plans for me! Today I talk with many people who are just beginning. They typically feel as inadequate for the task as I once did. But I want to encourage you by saying you will learn a lot—if you are teachable—and your confidence will grow as you do.

Your volunteers must be teachable, too. God has placed you in your position, even if by default. With the position comes the authority to make decisions regarding how classes will be set up, how programs will be administered, and whether or not you will hold teacher training meetings. So set your standards high! Expect your volunteers to respond with teachable spirits and great enthusiasm. In my ten years as Children's Director I've learned that people with high-quality skills often volunteer to work with children. But if they do not have a teachable spirit, it probably means they would be more effective in some other area of ministry.

*Have you made training a requirement?* I challenge you to make teacher training a requirement for ministering to children. (See *The Recruiting Remedy*, Judy Wortley, David C. Cook Pub. Co., for a complete teacher packet and requirements for teaching.) The subject of required training can become a natural part of your initial conversation with new volunteers. If a potential teacher balks at the requirement, simply say "Perhaps God has another area of ministry for you." I understand how hard that is when you need people so badly in your ministry, but don't settle for second best! God will meet your needs. The children of your church are too valuable to leave them in the hands of untrained teachers.

If you do set the standard by making teacher training a requirement for teaching, then you will lose some people that you think you cannot live without. But you *can* live without them! And God will replace them with others who are eager to do the best job possible.

Pray for His direction and His grace will abound to you more and more! God places high standards on us and we can do no less for those we are shepherding.

## Review Your Plans

Of course, you want to be sure everything is ready for your first meeting.

The confidence you have in what you are teaching
will flow through to your volunteers and make
a big difference in the confidence they place in you.

Even though you can't *guarantee* that everything will go smoothly or exactly the way you planned, you can do your best to forestall any potential problems.

*Check your materials.* All of your lesson materials should be in the room well before the meeting begins, including all pre-session materials like construction paper, pens, tape, etc. You will want to have these distributed on the chairs with instructions on the overhead projector so participants can get involved as soon as they enter the room.

Have your handouts ready to distribute, too. Using one or more handouts will give your participants a tangible way to recall what took place at the meeting. It will give them the opportunity to be involved. Your handout can consist of buzz group discussion questions, a sheet for note taking with fill-in blanks, reminders of policies, etc.

Check all your materials and lesson plans to be sure you are confident in your own spirit regarding what will be taking place that evening. This should perhaps be done even before the day of the meeting. The confidence you have in what you are teaching will flow through to your volunteers and make a big difference in the confidence they place in you.

**Note:** During some meetings, take time to have your teachers survey the condition of their rooms. Things tend to pile up as the weeks go by. Old curriculum, broken toys, scraps of craft materials, and "lost and found" items need to be tended to. (See **Resource 24** for a way to organize this ongoing "house cleaning" task.)

*Check your attitude.* It is true, you are the leader of this group of people called the Children's Ministry Team. They will be looking to you for leadership and you have the awesome responsibility to help them become more successful. But being the leader of a team does not give us the authority to think of ourselves more highly than we ought (see Romans 12:3).

Jesus gave us the prime example of how to be a servant: "Who, being in very nature God, did not consider equality with God something to be grasped, but made himself nothing, taking the very nature of a servant, being made in human likeness" (Philippians 2:6, 7). In Matthew 20:26 Jesus tells us: "Whoever wants to be great among you must be your servant." Thus, as we come before our volunteers, let us exhibit the attitude of a servant. It is your responsibility to help them become successful!

Helping someone else be successful takes lots of patience. Many are slow to respond. An attitude of tenacity will pay

> You may want to decorate for the meeting . . . . It is
> a real treat for a group to come to meetings
> never knowing what they will find.

you large dividends. It took very slow, painstaking efforts to convince the volunteers under my care that they would benefit from regular teacher training. But by being persistent, encouraging, and always well-prepared, I found that people did respond. Eventually they began looking forward to each teacher training meeting as a new adventure in spiritual growth.

## Prepare the Room

When you enter a room for a meeting you immediately have some kind of an emotional response. You start feeling relaxed or you tense up a little. For example, the lighting and the room temperature can be either inviting or distracting.

*Make it inviting.* Experts are hired today to create all kinds of atmospheres—from decorating doctor's offices to putting the right colors in a church. The environment makes a big difference in our willingness to return to a place. If your meeting room is junky or dirty, you may get a reaction like: "This meeting must not be too important; the room didn't even get cleaned!"

A bad odor can cause undue stress. Rooms with musty smells or those close to the back door garbage will detract from what we might have learned in a meeting. Consider purchasing an electric potpourri simmering pot to help create a pleasant atmosphere for your special meeting.

Your meeting room should be well-lighted, clean, and the right temperature. If the room you are assigned does not meet these criteria, you should make every effort to transform the room into a warm, friendly, good-smelling place.

Hang all visuals that will be used on the walls. Occasionally, during holiday times, you may want to decorate for the meeting with streamers or other fun things on the walls. It is a real treat for a group to come to meetings never knowing what they will find. Helium balloons, streamers, party hats occasionally, party favors. . . . Come on—get creative! These are people who work with kids! Give it a party atmosphere.

I recommend having your theme verse or philosophy statement on a large banner. It should be hung prior to the meeting time. It will reinforce the whole purpose for children's ministry. A large poster with the reasons for teacher training could also be hung. Put up key words or pictures that pertain to the technique training for the meeting. (Remember, a volunteer could be utilized to help you with these kinds of details.)

Never hesitate to ask your group members to get up and move their chairs to a different position during the evening. Keep them guessing . . .

*Be creative with chairs and tables.*
Set up less chairs than people you expect. There is something psychologically pleasing about walking into a room in which all the chairs are filled or nearly full. It says: " Wow! This must be a good meeting!" But walking into a room that seats twenty-five people, and finding only five chairs occupied makes us wonder why "nobody" showed up!

Don't arrange your chairs the same for every meeting. Put them in small semi-circles, squares, short rows, divided into two groups or four groups—depending, of course, on the activities you are using during the evening. You may have chairs labeled on certain meeting nights if you want the pre-school and elementary teachers to all sit in the same area.

Never hesitate to ask your group members to get up and move their chairs to a different position during the evening. Keep them guessing so they never know what to expect when they arrive at one of your meetings.

*Remember refreshment details.*
Don't forget to set up the coffee pot, tea, and refreshment table. It is a good idea to use a tablecloth; don't leave the table bare. The warmth of a cloth makes a big difference in the general feeling of the room. You may have a refreshment chairperson to take care of these details for you.

The idea is to have refreshments ready early, so the coffee or tea is ready to drink when the first person arrives. Put out on the table a basket or holiday decanter with some mini-candy bars, tiny bags of peanuts, or individually wrapped candy for volunteers to pick up as they sign in and get a cup of coffee. Don't forget cups, napkins, cream, sugar, and spoons. A flat basket or tray with the packaged creamer, sugar, and plastic stir spoons can just be spruced up from month to month if you keep it tucked away for use at each meeting.

Be sure all arrangements have been made for the actual serving of refreshments. If you will be the one doing the serving, be sure to gather your paper plates, bowls, utensils, and whatever else you may need. Have your refreshments out of sight until the time has come for them to be served to the group.

*Prepare name tags and sign-in sheet.*
Place your sign-in sheet on the refreshment table (see **Resource 25**). Asking people to sign in gives them a sense of being accountable to attend training meetings: you are making a record of their attendance; this must be an important event! Signing in let's them know you take the meeting seriously and

Because you are modeling what you want your teachers
to do in the classroom, it is very important that every aspect of
the meeting be an example of correct procedure.

intend for them to be accountable.

Have the name tags nearby so as people sign in they can fill out a name tag at the same time. Name tags give each person identity and will help all the team members get acquainted. Don't forget the pens and pins.

## Lead the Session

Now that you have gotten all the details taken care of, you are ready to think about how you will lead an interesting, productive training session. Here are the key steps:

*Arrive early.* Be in the meeting room when the first person arrives. NEVER be late to the meeting! Punctuality is a way of honoring those we serve. Because you are modeling what you want your teachers to do in the classroom, it is very important that every aspect of the meeting be an example of correct procedure.

Your volunteers should always be urged to arrive at least fifteen minutes before their first student arrives.

*Greet people warmly as they arrive.* You are the host/hostess. It's your party! Direct arrivals to the sign-in table. Ask them to get a name tag, sign in, get a cup of coffee, find a seat, and proceed with the pre-session

activity on the overhead projector. Again, you are modeling what you want teachers to do in the classroom.

*Begin on time.* As difficult as it may seem, you need to begin promptly at the scheduled time. Once your volunteers understand that you are a prompt beginner they will realize that if they arrive late they will be missing some important parts of the meeting. Remember—model the desired behavior!

*Open with prayer.* It is our obligation as leaders to let those we minister to see that we depend on God to bless our ministry, just as we want them to depend on His strength in the classroom. Asking God to direct your time together opens the way for each person to operate at his or her highest level during the meeting.

*Welcome with praise and enthusiasm.* Praising and encouraging your workers should be one of your most pleasant tasks. They are the lifeblood of all that you do. Without them you would not have a ministry. They are the hands, feet, eyes, ears, and loving arms that minister to the children. You could never accomplish your goals without these dear people. They are your "flock"—the flock God has called you to lead and care for. The monthly meeting is the perfect place to let them know just how special they are to you and to the children to whom they minister.

*Begin the technique training.* Introduce your guest lecturer, do a live demonstration with children, show a film, present a skit, or do the teaching yourself. Be as accurate and efficient as possible. Use lots of buzz groups and discussion so participants will have the opportunity to express themselves to you and to each other. Keep this portion of the meeting to about forty-five minutes.

*Give announcements.* There are always multitudes of housekeeping announcements to be made. (Keep a list during the month of various things you want to communicate to the entire group, otherwise you may forget some important information.) However, you need to make only those announcements that pertain to the entire group. These might include policies for checking out supplies, taking attendance, special prayer requests, or other matters that involve everyone. Don't waste everyone's time with items that apply to only a few people or one department. Use the announcement time to drop in

short little inspirational messages. Every chance you get, let your workers know they are special people!

*Award prizes for perfect attendance.* Awarding prizes helps make your meetings fun and full of frolic—not bedlam, just fun. Let your creative mind govern what you will be giving out and to what groups. You may reward entire classrooms with all their teachers in attendance at the meeting. You may want to give prizes to the department leaders if they have their entire departments present. This shifts some of the accountability to individual volunteers to be at the meeting so they won't let their departments down.

If your church doesn't have departments, you will still have various rooms that have two or more teachers. Think of some ways to reward them for coming to the meetings. Whether you have five teachers—or five hundred—you should be able to make them feel special. After all, they are the heart of your ministry!

At some meetings I worked it out for everyone to take something special home. Once I served homemade ice cream. I found some sturdy pastel ice cream scoops at a discount store and gave one to each person.

This is the time to give out Second-Miler buttons, special attendance certificates, or special achievement awards. The prizes can be as creative as you want to make them—screwdrivers for the men, fancy bars of soap for the women, or maybe gift certificates for hot-fudge sundaes.

*Have a social time.* This is a significant time for your group members. Many of them are giving up a Sunday school class for themselves to work with children. They really appreciate being able to come together. Twice a year or so you may want to hold a potluck dinner for them. This might include their families. A potluck can be held before the meeting, having family members exit when it is time for the meeting to begin. (**Note**: At the beginning of your social time, use fifteen or twenty minutes for some get-acquainted games. Some of the games could even be physically lively to help people "loosen up.")

Other suggestions for special social times during the year might include: an appreciation dessert or dinner; an appreciation barbecue; an open house at Christmas, or a Thanksgiving potluck. During the summer months consider having a swim party or a time in the park together. Including families is a great way to help volunteers feel more like they are part of a team. Any of these special events would probably take the

place of your regular teacher training for that month.

*Serve refreshments.* As refreshments are served by a committee or person that you have appointed for this, you will have the chance to mingle, say "Hello," and express your appreciation. Try not to use this time for problem solving. If people need to discuss a specific concern, tell them you will be coming around to their rooms in just a few minutes.

As you announce the serving of refreshments, you should also tell your group members to go directly to their departmental meetings as soon as they are finished eating.

*Adjourn to classrooms for departmental meetings.* Every room in your Sunday school needs to be prepared for Sunday morning. It doesn't matter if you have 3 or 4 rooms with only a half-dozen children, preparation will still give your teachers the confidence they need to help every child feel the love of Jesus. Without preparation, teachers will lose control of the room because they have run out of things to do, or the kids will be bored waiting for them to tear out their craft papers or other preparations. If you have only a few children in each room there should

> ### Never try to remember something
> ### someone needs without writing it down.

still be two adults in every room. It is much too discouraging to teach alone. In the case of an emergency, there should be one adult available to go for help.

One of the greatest assets to teacher training is the time allotted for individuals to do their planning for the next month. During this time plans should be made for each teacher's individual responsibility during the coming four weeks. Plans should be made as to what crafts will be done, what music will be used, and so forth. Most all curriculum provides specific instructions for all areas of the morning, but it is so helpful for each volunteer to know exactly what is expected of him or her for the coming month. All separations of Sunday school take-home papers should be done during this time. Manila folders labeled with the Sunday of the month the papers will be used, are helpful in sorting out papers, making them ready for use the moment they are needed.

 *Visit each classroom to discuss individual class needs.* There will always be something each teacher needs to discuss with you regarding problem children, or lesson planning, or something about the physical layout of the classroom. If you have more than one department using a room, take this opportunity to discuss the transition from one hour to the next. Departments

may choose to meet in opposite ends of the room for their planning time. Give as much time as you can to each concern, but don't linger in the rooms or you will not make it around to each one.

Always carry a clipboard with you to write down the myriad details you will be asked to remember. Never try to remember something someone needs without writing it down. If you can't write it down, ask the person to call you at your office or at home to remind you. I always cautioned my volunteers: "If you don't see me write it down, don't plan on getting it done."

 *Mail "I-missed-you" cards.* Do this on the morning after the meeting. Use your sign-in sheet. People who did not call to let you know they would not be at the meeting should be sent a card indicating that you missed them. You may want to telephone certain volunteers to find out the reason for their absence (see **Resource 26**). Be certain your card or telephone call expresses a *genuine* loss because of their absence, *not a condemnation* for missing the meeting. Generate a spark of interest by telling them how special the meeting was, perhaps highlighting some significant event of the evening.

 *Highlight the meeting in your Children's Ministry Newsletter.*

*There will be days when you wonder, "Why am I doing this?"*
*But that question has some very good answers . . .*

Everyone will be reminded of the topic discussed and those that missed the meeting will realize they really missed out.

## Evaluate Your Efforts

Evaluation is a healthy process for any activity we want to improve upon—especially in the areas of our ministry that have the potential to bear eternal fruit. Most of the time we are able to evaluate what we have done ourselves. Use **Resource 27** to help in evaluating your meetings. It would also be helpful from time to time to have someone else on the staff or on the children's ministry team do an evaluation of the meeting time. Our blind spots keep us from seeing areas we could improve upon. Keep an open heart and mind as you plan for each training time. These meetings will be one of the keys to loving and maintaining your volunteers!

## Don't Give Up

Sound like a lot of work? It is! Yet your successful training meetings can become the highlight of your month as God uses you to motivate volunteers to new levels of expertise and commitment.

Yes, there will be days of discouragement when you have planned so much and so few people come to a meeting.

There will be days when you wonder, "Why am I doing this?" But that question has some very good answers: Because God has called you to be the very best for Him that you can possibly be; because your recruiting will be made lighter as your volunteers are trained better; because the more confident your workers are, the more their teaching will become a life-style, a life-style that will last a lifetime.

To get you started, I have planned a meeting for you. It begins on page 57. This is a meeting that will jog even the veteran into evaluating her/his own methods of operation. It's a simple meeting for you to use as it is, or to add your own creative ideas. It will begin you on your way to great teacher training.

Once you get started, keep pressing on! The Lord will reward your perseverance. If you feel discouragement creeping in, remember these beautiful words: "Let us not become weary in doing good, for at the proper time we will reap a harvest if we do not give up" (Galatians 6:9).

# Taking the next step:

Start thinking about your next meeting!

Meeting time: _____ Date: _____

Location: _____

Topic: _____

Fill in the outline of your meeting on Resource 28. What objectives do you have for your time together? Be specific: _____

_____

_____

What should you be praying about between now and then?

_____

_____

_____

_____

In the space below, make a "thumbnail sketch" of one or two handouts you could use in your next meeting:

After the meeting:
I have gone through the Evaluation Checklist in Resource 27: **YES  NO**

# BACK TO THE BASICS TRAINING MEETING

**AIM:** The aim of this meeting is to motivate volunteers to teach with purpose. It will review with them the basics of good teaching habits, giving them the impetus to remove stress from their role as Sunday school teacher. The meeting should motivate them to be all they can be in ministering to their students.

**PREPARATION:**  ❑ One copy of **Resources 7, 28, 31**
    ❑ Overhead transparency of **Resource 29**
    ❑ Overhead projector, screen, projector table
    ❑ Copies of **Resources 30** and **31** for each person at the meeting
    ❑ Refreshments
    ❑ Sign-in sheet (**Resource 25**) with pens
    ❑ Name tag for each person with pins (use **Resource 9**)
    ❑ Optional: Icebreaker game (copies of **Resource 11** or **12** for each person)

**TO BEGIN:**  Read through this entire lesson so you will get a general idea of what this meeting will be about.

Then complete **Resources 7** and **28**.

--------------------------------------------------------------------------------

## PRE-SESSION ACTIVITY: (10 Minutes)

As your volunteers arrive, be sure to greet them warmly and have the coffee/drinks on the table with a finger food they can easily pick up and take to their seats. Be sure you have the sign-in sheet close at hand for them to use and the name tags with pens on the snack table.

Set your chairs up in circles of about 4-5. On each chair place a 3 X 5 card with a pen for each person to use. Have the instructions (**Resource 29**) on the overhead projector so people may begin the moment they sit down.

**OPTIONAL:**  Play one of the icebreaker games found in **Resources 11** and **12**.

## WELCOME: (5 Minutes)

Welcome volunteers with enthusiasm and open with a word of prayer. Ask God for His will and blessing to be seen throughout the evening.

Let volunteers know how happy you are that they have made the effort to come to this meeting. Tell them the meeting will be worth their efforts and God will richly increase their ministry because of their teachable hearts and openness to learn all they can about teaching in the special class God has placed them.

## TRUE/FALSE QUIZ: (15-25 Minutes)

Hand out the True/False Quiz (**Resource 30**). Ask people to work through the quiz individually. Allow 5 minutes for them to complete the quiz.

After they have finished the quiz. Go through each question, giving the answers and the rationale for each answer. If there's time, ask a few questions along the way. Keep the discussion moving.

### 1. Answer is FALSE

Tell them about the necessity for being well prepared. The well-prepared teacher will have much less chaos in the classroom. Discipline problems will be minimized dramatically. Talk about the necessity of having all crafts prepared and curriculum sheets torn from the books in advance— ready to be handed out. Caution against teachers and helpers standing at the counter preparing these things after children arrive. If children are left without something to do, or they sense the teacher is preoccupied, this is the time when major discipline problems begin. Good preparation prevents most problems that will arise.

**Ask:** What tips do you have for being well prepared?

### 2. Answer is TRUE

The teacher's manual can be left at home on Sundays. Teachers should know the materials and the outline of the lesson so well that the teacher's manual would not even be necessary to have on hand. Give your teachers encouragement for teaching from the Bible. The Bible should always be held when teaching children. The teacher's guide should be put away (a 3 X 5 card can be placed in the Bible for notes) and the Bible should be the book used to teach. Teach your people to talk to the children about God's Book. Have them remind the children God's Book is true. Train them to teach directly from the Bible. Children are literal! If you say the Bible says thus and so,

they should see you using the Bible to teach, not the teacher's guide.

### 3. Answer is FALSE

Children should not be allowed to disrupt the rest of the children. In the preschool age it is often common for them to raise their hand in the middle of a story to ask a totally unrelated question or to ask to have a drink or go to the bathroom. Preschoolers may not understand the disruptiveness behind some of their actions. Preschoolers can, however, lovingly be taught to wait until the proper time to talk and not interrupt. This lesson is not designed to give teachers a lesson on the characteristics of children but to be an encourager. Therefore, your comments at this time will be limited. All our children should learn to understand that being attentive shows the worth of other people. Attentiveness is showing the worth of a person by giving sincere attention to his or her words. Elementary-age children should always be asked to give their attention to what is happening within the classroom. Sometime you may want to schedule a training meeting on the art of storytelling or Bible learning activities. Your volunteers will get excited about planning the hour. Again emphasize that great preparation will allow workers to keep the children's attention much more easily.

**Ask:** What might you say to children who are being disruptive?

## 4. Answer is FALSE

The Lord has placed great value on knowing people's names and we should also. A person who calls you by name is a person you relate to and remember! Volunteers should learn and know all their students' names. You may suggest placing a picture of each student in an album along with the name for teachers and helpers to look at and use to pray for each child. Always provide name tags for teachers and helpers to use at class throughout the year, particularly when new students are coming to class. Stick-on tags should also be handy for any visitors.

## 5. Answer is FALSE

Obviously if both of the volunteers had this attitude there would be some Sundays that both of them would be late. Being on time means you are in the room ready and prepared BEFORE the first student arrives. This should be part of every teacher's commitment to the children. Volunteers need to be prepared to arrive ten to fifteen minutes before class begins.

## 6. Answer is FALSE

Encourage volunteers to begin preparation on Sunday afternoon of each week. Reading lessons a week ahead gives God the opportunity to bring us into a personal experience with the content of the lesson.

**Ask:** When do you prepare lessons?

## 7. Answer is TRUE

You may have some folks disagree with you on this question; however, it has been proven throughout the world by many organizations that meeting a person's physical needs opens the way for him or her to receive the Gospel. Jesus, Himself, met the physical needs of people on many occasions prior to presenting the Gospel to them. We know a starving person would not want to hear of Jesus' love in place of a loaf of bread. Jesus calls us to meet the physical needs of people as well as their spiritual needs! Children who come to our classrooms, are for the most part well fed and clothed. Even so children who are too cold, too hot, wet, or fearful will not be responsive to the words we have for them if those physical and emotional needs are not dealt with first.

**Ask:** What needs do your students have?

## 8. Answer is TRUE

In Matthew 10:24 Jesus says that a student will become like his teacher.

**Ask:** What does this verse say about our responsibility as teachers?

## 9. Answer is FALSE

Most of our major discipline problems occur when the structure of the classroom is loose. Young children, as well as elementary-age children want parameters set for them. They actually respond better and carry out instruction better when they are in a controlled environment. If the volunteer feels it is absolutely necessary to give them social time, then allow a few minutes at the very end of the class time. It is better to keep good control during the hour and give them a short time at the end to visit. Most of their visiting can be done before or after class is in session.

## 10. Answer is FALSE

Our goal is for our students to get into the Bible for themselves! We want to create a thirst and hunger in them that will cause them to want to get into Scripture for themselves—at home and times other than at Sunday school. Getting the Bible into them may be something that helps us feel we have done our duty for the week, but our primary goal should be to teach them to love God's Word and get into it on their own.

## 11. Answer is FALSE

Teacher training should be so exciting and so filled with encouragement that no volunteer would want to miss these meetings. They should be mandatory to teaching. Teacher training is also a gift to students as teachers are better prepared to teach them. This would be a good opportunity to review the benefits of teacher training.

## 12. Answer is FALSE

Good, solid curriculum cannot be replaced within the classroom. Curriculum gives scope and sequence to everything you are doing. Curriculum gives us the confidence of knowing that each student will be taken through the entire Bible. It gives continuity and accountability to what is being taught within each class.

As you answer this question help your volunteers to see how important it will be to their students to stay on target by using the provided curriculum. Certainly curriculum can be adapted, but rarely should entire lessons be thrown out at the whim of the teacher.

**Ask:** How can you adapt your curriculum to best meet the needs of your students?

## 13. Answer is FALSE

Every class needs to have two people in the room, no matter how small the class may be. Refer to Ecclesiastes 4:9, 10. It can be very discouraging to teach a class alone. Besides offering enouragement, a partner allows for each person to have someone to be there in case of an emergency. Unfortunately, in today's culture, it is also safer for accountability reasons to have two people teaching, even if there are only two children.

## 14. Answer is FALSE

Common courtesy would give us the answer to this question. However, I am always amazed that there have been those who simply failed to let anyone know they would be gone on a particular Sunday. You will want to let the volunteers all know about your substitute list. (If you don't have one, you need to develop an approved substitute list for them to use in calling their substitutes.) Train them to replace themselves while they are gone and to let you know in advance they will be absent from their usual place on Sunday. Go through your procedures for when someone plans to be away.

## 15. Answer is FALSE

Studies show that all ages learn better in the correct environment. It has been proven within the classroom that color stimulates the mind to learning. A clean, neat classroom is part of taking care of students' physical needs. The rooms need to smell great—and look great! A clean, neat classroom says, "I care!" New, fresh bulletin boards and visuals on the walls show that things are happening in that room. Jesus said let the children come to Me; He took them in His arms and blessed them. He gave them priority! Our classrooms should reflect our priority!

## 16. Answer is TRUE

A child learns something the moment he enters the room. He learns who is in control. If there is no one in the room, or the room is chaotic, the child can quickly gain control. The teacher needs to be in control from the moment the first child enters the room. It remains, therefore, of utmost importance for the teacher to be prepared and to enroll the child in creative learning the moment the child enters the room.

**Ask:** What tips do you have for getting students involved as soon as they enter the classroom?

## ACT IT OUT: (10-15 Minutes)

Distribute the Back to the Basics sheet (**Resource 31**) to each person. Then make the skit assignments from **Resource 32** to four groups. Give groups 6 minutes to prepare their skit to present to the entire group. If you do not have that many teachers available at the meeting, pick one of the skits and have those present act out the one you have chosen. If you have a small teaching staff, why not ask some of the high school students ahead of time to prepare and present each of the four skits for the volunteers.

Have your skits presented, and then call for a large group discussion of what they saw and what impressed them about the topics chosen.

## ANNOUNCEMENTS: (5 Minutes)

Make all announcements pertinent to the entire group. This will include all prizes to be given out or special awards.

## CLASSROOM MEETINGS:

Adjourn all classes to go to their individual rooms for their monthly planning.

## TOMORROW:

Choose one of the cards from **Resource 26** and mail to those who missed the meeting. Write something personal on each card so they know you genuinely realize they were gone.

*"No, it's not our tax refund, Honey. It's an invitation to the next Teacher Training Meeting."*

# RESOURCES

# SUNDAY MORNING CLASSROOM PLANNER

| TIME | TEACHER | Sandy | Joe | Judy |
|------|---------|-------|-----|------|
| 8:30–9:00 | Arrive—be sure there are sign in sheets. Get out Make-It-Take-It papers, bottom right cabinet under sink. Put puzzles out on tables nearest puzzles. Toys on table near sink.<br><br>– – – – – – – – –<br><br>Greet each child entering. | Try to arrive as close to 8:45 as possible. Work with children at puzzle table or toy table as needed. Or take and comfort a child who is scared or crying. | Go to block area or home living center—help children play there and try to relate discussion to today's lesson. | Arrive and do craft with children. |
| 9:00–9:15 | Continue greeting—let others do other things. | Continue above | Continue above | ↓ |
| 9:15 | Clean up. All children go to teacher near door #13, sing a couple of songs as they come in. | Help clean up and encourage children to join group. | Same as other helper<br>← | Finish any craft cleanup. |
| about 9:20 | Dismiss blue group to go outside with others. Yellow group can then go to tables. Begin story time with red group. | Lay out papers (Make-It-Take-It) and crayons on table by cubby holes and one by the sink. Set at one table and explain paper, then let them do it. They will need to know what it's about and how to do it. Encourage neatness. | Outside<br>blue group | Same as other helper or outside. |
| Bell or signal | Send children to tables. Open door behind you and blue group will enter for story time. | Send children to door #12 to wait for helper. Begin red group. | Outside<br>yellow | Outside |
| | Repeat for yellow. | Repeat for blue. | Repeat for red. | Outside |
| about 10:05 song-time | Put last group of Make-It-Take-Its in cubby holes with a story card. Put podium at door. | Put out puzzles on one table, coloring on one table and books. | Help keep children involved. | Same as other helper<br>←<br>or help set up. |

# SUNDAY MORNING CLASSROOM PLANNER

| TIME | TEACHER | | | |
|------|---------|---|---|---|
|      |         |   |   |   |

# REASONS FOR TEACHER TRAINING

*To Impart Vision*

*To Build Team Spirit*

*To Offer Encouragement*

*To Provide Social Time*

*To Equip Volunteers*

# MONTHLY PLANNING CALENDAR

## SEPTEMBER

22nd—"Intro night"

Movie:
    Cipher in the Snow
    1 to 1 Relationship with
        Kids

## OCTOBER

27th
    Lou
    Bina
    Townsend
    "STORY TELLING"

31st—Pumpkin patch

## NOVEMBER

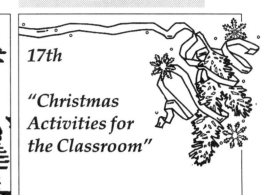

17th

"Christmas
Activities for
the Classroom"

## DECEMBER

12th — OPEN HOUSE AT JUDY'S

18th—Children's Musical

## JANUARY

26th
"Effective Use of Puppets"

## FEBRUARY

23rd
✷✷ Live Demonstrations

<u>Introducing New Students</u>
with Kathy Howell
<u>Discipline</u> with Bev Long
12th—Teacher Appreciation
19th—Missions Faire

## MARCH

15th
"Easter
Activities
for the
Classroom"

30th—"Donut Man"

## APRIL

27th
    "Learning Centers"
    with Marie Kenyon

## MAY

25th
    "Spring Cleaning"

Homemade Ice Cream!

## JUNE

## JULY

SUMMER

## AUGUST

24th
    "Fall Planning"

# MONTHLY PLANNING CALENDAR

You may photocopy this page for ministry use.

# TWO SUGGESTED MEETING SCHEDULES

*PLAN A*

*6:45-7:00*  COFFEE, TEA, SIGN-IN SHEETS,
NAME TAGS, PRE-SESSION SNACK ON TABLE

GREET VOLUNTEERS AS THEY ARRIVE

PRE-SESSION ACTIVITY

*7:00-7:05*  OPEN IN PRAYER/WELCOME

*7:05-7:50*  TECHNIQUE TRAINING

*7:50-8:00*  ANNOUNCEMENTS/ENCOURAGEMENT

*8:00-8:20*  SOCIAL/GAME TIME

*8:20-8:40*  REFRESHMENTS

*8:40-9:40*  DEPARTMENTAL MEETINGS


*PLAN B*

*6:45-7:00*  COFFEE, TEA, SIGN-IN SHEETS,
NAME TAGS, PRE-SESSION SNACK ON TABLE

WELCOME

PRE-SESSION ACTIVITY

*7:00-8:00*  DEPARTMENTAL PLANNING

*8:00-8:05*  OPEN IN PRAYER/WELCOME

*8:05-8:15*  ANNOUNCEMENTS/ENCOURAGEMENT

*8:15-8:35*  SOCIAL/GAME TIME

*8:35-8:55*  REFRESHMENTS

*8:55-9:40*  TECHNIQUE TRAINING

**RESOURCE 7**

# TRAINING MEETING PLANNING SHEET

DATE:_____SUBJECT:_____

INSTRUCTOR/FILM:_____

AUDIOVISUAL EQUIPMENT: PROJECTION TABLE:_____EXTENSION CORD:_____

FILM:_____FILMSTRIP:_____SLIDES:_____OVERHEAD:_____SCREEN:_____VCR:____

DATE RESERVED:_____FROM WHERE:_____

PRE-SESSION ACTIVITIES:_____

PRE-SESSION MATERIALS:_____

WALL VISUALS:_____

PERSON MAKING THEM:_____

PRE-SESSION SNACK:_____

REFRESHMENTS:_____

DRINKS:_____

PREPARED BY:_____PHONE NO._____

SERVED BY:_____PHONE NO._____

DECORATIONS/NAPKINS:_____

TYPE OF NAME TAGS:_____

PREPARED BY:_____PHONE NO._____

PRIZES TO BE GIVEN OUT:_____

GIVEN TO:_____

GAMES:_____

GAME MATERIALS NEEDED:_____

ANNOUNCEMENTS:_____

_____

# CHECKLIST FOR MEETING PREPARATION

Today's Date_____ Meeting Date_____

Subject_____

## I Have:

❑ Outlined my lesson activities
_____
_____
_____

❑ Chosen prizes to give away
_____
_____
_____

❑ Prepared any necessary handouts
_____
_____
_____

❑ Decided what announcements are needed
_____
_____
_____

❑ Gathered material for presession activities
_____
_____
_____

❑ Prepared name tags
_____
_____
_____

❑ Collected visual aids/films or videos
_____
_____
_____

❑ Decided on room decorations
_____
_____
_____

❑ Collected necessary AV equipment
_____
_____
_____

❑ Sent flyer
_____
_____
_____

❑ Planned for refreshments
_____
_____
_____

❑ Informed people in other ways
_____
_____
_____

❑ Prepared any games
_____
_____
_____

❑ Made reminder calls
_____
_____
_____

❑ Prayed about the meeting!

# NAME TAGS

Create your own name tags by cutting and pasting the various items in the left hand column inside the blank borders on the right. Make as many photocopies as you need.

## CMT

CHILDREN'S MINISTRY

CHILDREN'S MINISTRY TEAM

SUNDAY SCHOOL

MID-WEEK PROGRAM

CHILDREN'S CHURCH

CHILDREN'S CHOIR

HELPER

TEACHER

AGE GROUP:

## VBS

# HOLIDAY NAME TAGS

# Find someone who . . .

owns a dog _____

_____ wears contact lenses

was born outside the U.S.A. _____

_____ has red hair

is wearing brown socks _____

_____ has been in Canada

is bald _____

_____ has/had a mother who taught Sunday school

has owned a motorcycle _____

_____ owns a Volkswagen

has been in the cockpit of an airplane _____

_____ has had more than three traffic tickets

has eaten frog legs _____

_____ didn't know your last name

has never had chicken pox _____

_____ has a moustache

is wearing red _____

_____ uses Close-Up Toothpaste

has popped popcorn in the last 30 days _____

_____ has never been out of our state

was born in our city _____

_____ has held a grandchild this week

is wearing a white sweater _____

_____ is wearing a Timex

# LET'S GET ACQUAINTED!

1. Get the signatures of the following people!

   1._____ a person you have known before.

   2._____ a person you do not know.

   3._____ a person who is attending teacher training for the first time.

   4._____ a person who teaches in his/her child's class.

   5._____ a person who does not have a child in the childrens' ministry.

   6._____ a person who also works as a teacher.

2. Find out the following information from one person in this room you did not know before today.

   Name_____

   Birthplace_____

   Hobby_____

   Occupation_____

   Grade level:_____

3. Locate three other people. Be seated and share the above information about yourself in 90 seconds or less.

*Your Church Name Here*

*Your City & State*

*This Certifies That*

has given exceptional service
above and beyond the call of duty
and is hereby awarded this

*Certificate*
*of*
*Appreciation*

on this _____ day of _____ 19 ___

_____
*Pastor*

You may photocopy this page for ministry use.

# SECOND-MILER BUTTONS

# APRIL
### Teacher Training
### APRIL 22 — 7:00 P.M.

The meeting will begin promptly at 7:00 p.m. in YOUR ROOM (the room in which you minister to the children each Sunday).

At 8:00 p.m. <u>sharp</u>, we will be sharing in a team-effort social time, followed by our topic, "Building Staff Relationships" in Room 4.

Please remember how important these meetings are to the entire team effort. You should consider them mandatory!

In His Service,

*Judy*

Judy Wortley
Director of Children's
Ministries

✳Prizes for Perfect
Attendance!
✳Coffee, Tea, &
Goodies!

## Mark It On Your Calendar!

# "Building Self-Esteem"

## April 26

Please join us as we explore the world of **"Self-Esteem in a Child."** Janelle Gibbs will give us insights as we learn the role of the teacher in the classroom, and the vital part *you* play in developing esteem in your students. "You can make a difference!"

See you at 7:00 p.m. in Room 4

## DEPARTMENT MEETINGS!

## REFRESHMENTS!

## FELLOWSHIP!

You may photocopy this page for ministry use.
Use the border and type in your own information.

# SING PRAISES TO THE
# LORD!

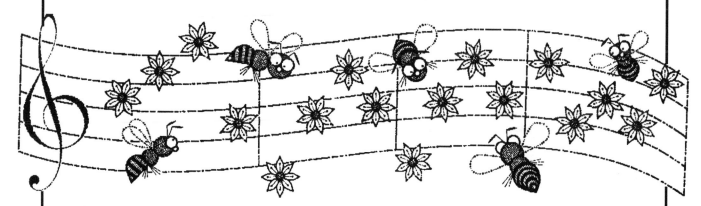

# (MUSIC IN THE SUNDAY SCHOOL)

Gladys Kerfoot and Melva Cookingham
will be sharing practical ways for
even the nonmusical person to
incorporate music into the
Sunday school classroom!

## JOIN US TUESDAY, MARCH 22,
## FOR TEACHER TRAINING AND FELLOWSHIP,
## 7:00 PM, IN ROOM 4.

Prizes for each department
with perfect attendance at the meeting.
*New and fun Easter prizes!*
BEE THERE!

In Christ,

*Judy*

Judy

## TEACHER TRAINING

will be Tuesday, February 23, at 7:00 P.M. in Room 4.

Easter Sunday is five weeks away. We will have an opportunity to minister to many children that morning. We want to share some fun activities you can do with your children in the classroom.

We will begin the evening with some Easter games! Don't be late!

Let me take this opportunity to tell you once again how vitally important it is to the entire ministry for you to attend Teacher Training. I deeply appreciate it when you do!

*See You There!*

In His Love and Joy,

*Judy*

Judy Wortley
Director of
Children's
Ministry

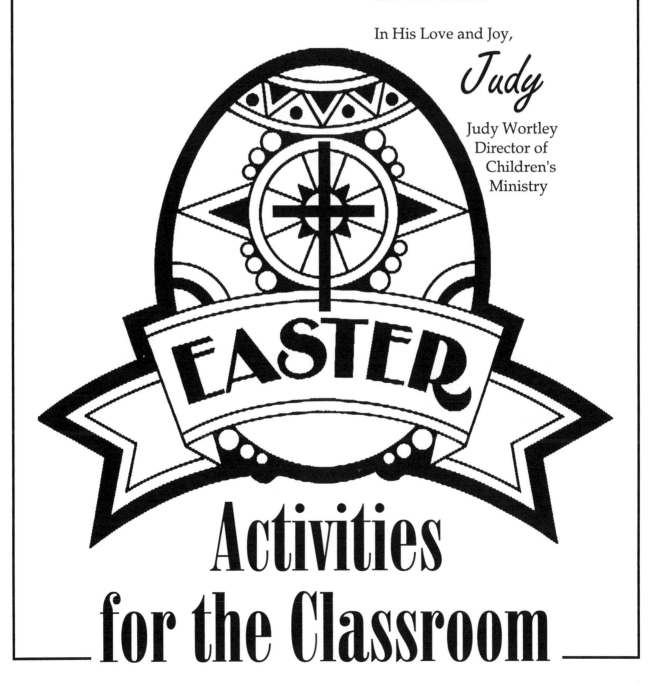

EASTER

Activities
for the Classroom

# It's Homemade Ice Cream Night!

## (& Spring House Cleaning!)

This month's meeting will be Tuesday, May 24, at 7:00 pm in Room 4.

It's time to once again spruce up our rooms and bulletin boards, clean our cupboards, and sort out our toys.

Please come prepared for a fun evening of work, fellowship and ice cream! You'll hear future plans for the fall and reflections on my three weeks away.

Don't miss it!!!

In Christ,

*Judy*

Judy

P.S. This will be our last meeting till late August. You will also be able to pick up your summer curriculum.

# CLIP ART—1

Clip art on this page courtesy of
Dynamic Graphics, Inc.
6000 N. Forest Park Drive
Peoria, IL 61614

Clip art on this page courtesy of
Dynamic Graphics, Inc.
6000 N. Forest Park Drive
Peoria, IL 61614

SUMMER

## PUNCTUALITY...

Is tied into your
commitment
to the
Lord.
We can't afford
to be late,
we serve a God
whose business
is urgent
and of utmost
importance.

WORLD'S Best

Clip art on this page courtesy of
Dynamic Graphics, Inc.
6000 N. Forest Park Drive
Peoria, IL 61614

# CLIP ART—4

# HOUSE CLEANING REPORT

ALL CLASSES USING THIS ROOM: PLEASE COMPLETE THIS SHEET TOGETHER

List any equipment, tables, chairs, faucets, etc. in need of repair.

List any supplies you need in your central supply in your room. (Scotch tape, crayons, pencils etc.)

List any new toys you would desire to have in your room.

Do you want your bulletin boards decorated?  Yes_____No_____

Do you want just butcher paper and border up?  Yes_____No_____

What color paper?_____

Please bring all throwaways, old curriculum, old bulletin board supplies, and broken toys to the Sunday School Office.

# SIGN-IN SHEET

Name:

_____

_____

_____

_____

_____

_____

_____

_____

_____

_____

_____

_____

_____

_____

_____

_____

_____

_____

_____

## I Missed You Cards

# EVALUATING THE MEETING

1. Were materials in the room before the meeting? Yes_____No_____

2. Did I greet people warmly? Describe my attitude._____

_____

3. Were the refreshments appropriate? and enough?_____

_____

4. What new information regarding teaching or being helped with their personal growth did teachers glean?_____

_____

_____

_____

_____

5. Describe my feelings about the whole evening._____

_____

_____

_____

_____

6. List any changes that need to be made next meeting._____

_____

_____

_____

_____

7. List any pertinent information I need to remember for future use, i.e., some significant event that a teacher shared with me._____

_____

# OUTLINE FOR TEACHER TRAINING MEETING

TIME_____

OPEN IN PRAYER_____

_____WELCOME_____

_____

_____

_____

_____LESSON OUTLINE_____

_____

_____

_____

_____

_____

_____

_____

_____

_____

_____

_____ANNOUNCEMENTS_____

_____

_____

_____

_____AWARD PRIZES_____

_____BEGIN GAMES_____

_____SERVE REFRESHMENTS_____

# WELCOME TO THE MEETING!

**Have a cup of coffee, sign in, grab a name tag, find a circle, and sit down!**

**Use the 3X5 card on your chair to write a paragraph describing your favorite teacher.**

**What did this teacher do that made him/her your favorite teacher?**

**Share with those in your circle what you have written.**

You may photocopy this page for ministry use. Use as an overhead or display at the sign-in table.

# TRUE/FALSE QUIZ

                                                                    **T**     **F**

1. The only real preparation I need for class is prayer.          _____  _____

2. It's okay to leave my teacher's guide at home on Sundays.      _____  _____

3. If 3 or 4 children are talking in the back row, it's
   better to continue telling the story than disrupt
   the thought pattern by speaking to them.                       _____  _____

4. As long as I know the children's faces I don't need
   to know their names.                                           _____  _____

5. As long as one teacher is in the room, it's okay for me
   to be late occasionally.                                       _____  _____

6. Saturday afternoon is the best time to start my lesson
   preparation, so it will be fresh on my mind.                   _____  _____

7. It's important to care for the children's physical needs
   before their spiritual needs.                                  _____  _____

8. The statement that a student becomes like his teacher
   was taught by Jesus.                                           _____  _____

9. It's good to give elementary children lots of free time
   at the beginning of class so they can talk to their friends.   _____  _____

10. I want to get the Bible into my students more than the
    students into the Bible.                                      _____  _____

11. I don't need to attend Teacher Training if it's going to
    be a real inconvenience.                                      _____  _____

12. If I don't like the curriculum one week, it's okay to
    do my own thing.                                              _____  _____

13. Since my class is so small, it's okay for me to be only
    teacher in the room.                                          _____  _____

14. If I'm going to be gone one Sunday, I don't need to
    find my own substitute. The rest of the department
    can do just fine without me.                                  _____  _____

15. Having a colorful and bright, clean, neat room, is not
    of primary importance.                                        _____  _____

16. Learning begins the moment a child enters the room.          _____  _____

# BACK TO THE BASICS

**B**E SURE TO PRAY FOR YOUR CLASS REGULARLY!

**A**RRIVE EARLY TO YOUR CLASSROOM!

**C**OME PREPARED!

**K**EEP YOUR PRE-SESSION FUN AND INVITING!

**T**EAM EFFORT WITH YOUR DEPARTMENT!

**O**RGANIZE YOUR MORNING SO EACH CHILD IS ALWAYS BUSY LEARNING!

**T**ELL THE STORY LESSON FROM MEMORY!

**H**AVE CRAFTS PREPARED AHEAD OF TIME!

**E**LIMINATE CHAOS FROM YOUR CLASSROOM THROUGH PREPARATION!

**B**AN NEGATIVE REMARKS FROM YOUR VOCABULARY!

**A**LERT YOURSELF TO THE NEEDS OF EACH CHILD!

**S**IT CLOSE TO THE CHILDREN, ON THEIR LEVEL!

**I**NVOLVE YOUR STUDENTS IN THE LEARNING PROCESS!

**C**ONSIDER EACH CHILD AS LOVED AND VALUED!

**S**ING HIS PRAISES, EVERMORE!

# SKIT NUMBER ONE

Using the statements on the BACK TO THE BASICS sheet, develop a skit showing all the things mentioned in the sentences that are with the word BACK. Show some of the negative/positive ways to do these things. Be sure to include lack of prayer, arriving late, coming unprepared and not having anything ready when the class arrives.

-----------------------------------------------------------------------------------------------------

# SKIT NUMBER TWO

Using the statements on the BACK TO THE BASICS sheet, develop a skit showing all the things mentioned in the statements attached to the word TO. Show some of the negative/positive ways to do these things. Be sure to include not getting along as a team and showing bored children getting into trouble because they have nothing to do.

-----------------------------------------------------------------------------------------------------

# SKIT NUMBER THREE

Using the statements on the BACK TO THE BASICS sheet, develop a skit showing all the things mentioned in the statements attached to the word THE. Show some of the negative/positive ways to do these things. Be sure to include reading the story from the teachers guide, having the crafts not prepared and children ruining the morning because they are running the room.

-----------------------------------------------------------------------------------------------------

# SKIT NUMBER FOUR

Using the statements on the BACK TO THE BASICS sheet, develop a skit showing all the things mentioned in the statements attached to the word BASICS. Show some of the negative/positive ways of doing these things. Be sure to include negative remarks, lack of sensitivity to the children, talking down to them, not letting them be involved and acting like you do not love and value them.

*Comments Joan receives about her training meetings*